Words from Wills

and other probate records
1500-1800

A Glossary

Stuart A. Raymond

Published by
The Federation of Family History Societies
Units 15-16, Chesham Industrial Estate
Oram Street, Bury
Lancashire, BL9 6EN

in association with
S.A. & M.J. Raymond
P.O. Box 35
Exeter, EX1 3YZ
Phone: 01392 (252193)
Email: samjraymond@btopenworld.com
Http: www.samjraymond.btinternet.co.uk/igb.htm

ISBNs:
Federation of Family History Societies: 1-86006-181-8
S.A. & M.J. Raymond: 1-899668-37-3

First published 2004

Printed and bound by The Alden Press, Osney Mead, Oxford, OX2 0EF

Contents

Front cover illustration: Sower with a seedlip.

Introduction

Wills and other probate records of the sixteenth to eighteenth centuries are vital sources for family and local historians, and have been used for a wide variety of purposes by modern researchers. They provide genealogists with much information on particular families, they enable local historians to re-construct the culture of the people who wrote them, and they give the basic data from which studies can be made of topics as diverse as furniture, literacy, and agriculture. The words used in them are, however, often no longer used in modern English, and may be difficult to understand for newcomers to historical research. Andirons, beres, and winding sheets were all very familiar items to our seventeenth-century ancestors, but the average person today would have no idea what they were.

The purpose of this book is to provide definitions for words commonly found in early modern probate records. It is based on a wide range of published collections of probate records, listed below. The glossaries in all of the editions listed have been compared and contrasted with each other, and with a number of specialist dictionaries (also listed below); the definitions given derive from this process. Where a word is likely to be localised, I have indicated the county in which it has been found, using the Chapman county code system of abbreviations, detailed on page 12. Such indications are intended as questions rather than authoritative statements.

Spelling during the period covered by this glossary was far from standardised. The same word could be spelt in many different ways. If an attempt were made to list all the variant spellings, the result would be a book twice as long as the present one. I have generally chosen that spelling which most closely corresponds to present-day usage. I have also tended to ignore the frequent addition of -e and -te suffixes to the ends of words, and the common substitution of y for i and e and vice versa, of c for t or s, f for v, *etc.* Variant spellings which are obvious, e.g. cownterfeit for counterfeit, truckel for truckle, trenchar for trencher, have not been listed. If you come across a word which seems not to be listed here, say it and then work out how you would spell it; you may well then be able to identify a definition. I have included a few variant spellings which might not be obvious, or which might be considered to be different words, perhaps influenced by dialect, e.g. cobberd for cob iron. I have not included definitions for words still in common use, except where their meanings have changed.

The words defined are arranged alphabetically, word by word. Where they consist of two words which are sometimes joined together, I have separated them, e.g. cap case, not capcase. Definitions for words which have several distinct meanings are numbered, so that they can be cross-referenced. Words which are defined elsewhere in the text are marked with an asterisk, and with a number if appropriate.

This glossary is confined to words used in probate records, and to their meanings in that context. Many other meanings are given in the *Oxford English dictionary,* and in Wright's *English dialect dictionary,* both of which have been checked for the words defined here.

The list of published probate records given below is not intended to be comprehensive, although it does include most modern editions (but only those with glossaries). Many other works on probate records are listed in my *English genealogy: a bibliography* (3rd ed., F.F.H.S., 1996), and in the county volumes of my *British genealogical library guides.*

Finally, a word of warning. Words used in probate records, and, indeed, in all historical records, must be understood in the light of their context.[1] Words can and do have different meanings in different contexts. A case in point is the word 'horse'. Three different definitions are offered below; a fourth meaning is not given because it is still in common use today. The researcher may need to give some thought to which meaning is intended. It is obviously important to avoid confusing a beast used for riding with a frame for drying clothes, or with trestles for a table. The context, however, will usually make it clear which is intended: riding beasts are most likely to be listed in inventories with other animals; trestles are likely to be with their associated table boards.

---

[1] For a full discussion of words and their contexts, see: TRINDER, BARRIE. 'The wooden horse in the cellar: words and their contexts in Shropshire Probate inventories', in ARKELL, TOM, EVANS, NESTA, & GOOSE, NIGEL, eds. *When death do us part: understanding and interpreting the probate inventories of early modern England.* Oxford: Leopards Head Press, 2000, pp. 268-84.

Acknowledgements

This book was typed by Cynthia Hanson and seen through the press by Bob Boyd. My thanks go to them and the officers of the Federation of Family History Societies, the publishers. It was inspired by the glossary I wrote for my Adelaide Unversity M.A. thesis (see p. 8), and the supervisor of that thesis, Professor Wilfrid Prest, also deserves thanks.

Stuart Raymond

Bibliography

DICTIONARIES

SIMPSON, J.A., & WEINER, E.S.C. *The Oxford English dictionary.* 2nd ed. 20 vols. Oxford: Clarendon Press, 1989.

HALLIWELL, JAMES ORCHARD. *A dictionary of archaic and provincial words, obsolete phrases, proverbs, and ancient customs from the fourteenth century.* 10th ed. 2 vols. John Russell Smith, 1887.

BRISTOW, JOY. *The local historians glossary and vade mecum.* 2nd ed. Nottingham: Dept. of Adult Education, University of Nottingham, 1994.

WRIGHT, JOSEPH, ed. *The English dialect dictionary, being the complete vocabulary of all dialect words still in use, or known to have been in use, during the last two hundred years.* 6 vols. Henry Frowde, 1898-1905.

COLLECTED EDITIONS

Bedfordshire

McGREGOR, MARGARET, ed. *Bedfordshire wills proved in the Prerogative Court of Canterbury, 1383-1548.* Publications of the Bedfordshire Historical Record Society, **58.** 1979.

BELL, PATRICIA, ed. *Bedfordshire wills, 1480-1519.* Publications of the Bedfordshire Historical Record Society, **45.** 1966.

BELL, PATRICIA L., ed. *Bedfordshire wills 1484-1533.* Publications of the Bedfordshire Historical Record Society, **76.** 1997.

COLLETT-WHITE, JAMES. *Inventories of Bedfordshire country houses 1714-1830.* Publications of the Bedfordshire Historical Society, **74.** 1995.

Buckinghamshire

REED, MICHAEL, ed. *Buckinghamshire probate inventories 1661-1714.* Buckinghamshire Record Society, **24.** 1988.

Cheshire

GROVES, JILL, ed. *Bowdon wills: wills and probate inventories from a Cheshire township.* 3 vols. Sale: Northern Writers Advisory Service, 1997. Pt.1. 1600-1650. Pt.2. 1651-1689. Pt.3. 1690-1760.

Cornwall

RAYMOND, S.A. *Seventeenth-century Week St. Mary, Cornwall, including an edition of the probate records 1598 to 1699.* M.A. thesis, University of Adelaide, 1988.

Derbyshire

MILWARD, ROSEMARY. *A glossary of household, farming and trade terms from probate inventories.* 2nd ed. Occasional paper, 1. Derbyshire Record Society, 1983.

Devon

CASH, MARGARET, ed. *Devon inventories of the sixteenth and seventeenth centuries.* Devon and Cornwall Record Society, new series, 11. 1966.

WYATT, PETER, ed. *The Uffculme wills and inventories, 16th to 18th centuries.* Devon and Cornwall Record Society, new series, **40**. 1997.

Dorset

MACHIN, R., ed. *Probate inventories and manorial excepts of Chetnole, Leigh and Yetminster.* [Bristol]: Dept. of Extra-Mural Studies, University of Bristol, 1976.

Durham

ATKINSON, J.A., et al, eds. *Darlington wills and inventories, 1600-1625.* Surtees Society, **201**. 1993.

Gloucestershire and Bristol

LANG, SHEILA, & McGREGOR, MARGARET, eds. *Tudor wills proved in Bristol, 1546-1603.* Bristol Record Society publication, **44**. 1993.

SALE, A.J.H., ed. *Cheltenham probate records, 1660-1740.* Gloucestershire record series, **12**. Bristol and Gloucestershire Archaeological Society, 1999.

MOORE, JOHN S., ed. *The goods and chattels of our forefathers: Frampton Cotterell and district probate inventories, 1539-1804.* Phillimore & Co., 1976.

Hampshire

ROBERTS, EDWARD, & PARKER, KAREN, eds. *Southampton probate inventories 1447-1575.* 2 vols. Southampton records series, **34-35**. 1992.

Hertfordshire

MUNBY, LIONEL M., ed. *Life & death in Kings Langley: wills and inventories, 1498-1659.* Kings Langley: Kings Langley Local History & Museum Society, 1981.

Lancashire

PHILLIPS, C.B., & SMITH, J.H., eds. *Stockport probate records, 1620-1650.* Record Society of Lancashire and Cheshire, 131. 1992.

Lincolnshire *See also* Yorkshire

FOSTER, C.W., ed. *Lincoln wills registered in the District Probate Registry at Lincoln, volume II: A.D. 1505 to May 1530.* Publications of the Lincoln Record Society, 10. 1918. Covers the whole county, not just Lincoln.

AMBLER, R.W., WATKINSON, B., & WATKINSON, L.A. *Farmers and fishermen: the probate inventories of the ancient parish of Clee, South Humberside, 1536-1742.* Studies in regional and local history, 4. Hull: University of Hull School of Adult and Continuing Education, 1987.

JOHNSTONE, J.A., ed. *Probate inventories of Lincoln citizens, 1661-1714.* Publications of the Lincoln Record Society, 80. 1991.

NEAVE, DAVID, ed. *Winteringham 1650-1760: life and work in a North Lincolnshire village, illustrated by probate inventories.* [Winteringham]: Winteringham W.E.A. Branch, 1984.

Norfolk

WILSON, J.H., ed. *Wymondham inventories.* Creative history from East Anglian sources, 1. Norwich: Centre of East Anglian Studies, 1993.

Nottinghamshire

KENNEDY, P.A., ed. *Nottinghamshire household inventories.* Thoroton Society record series, 22. 1963.

PERKINS, ELIZABETH R., ed. *Village life from wills & inventories: Clayworth parish, 1670-1710.* Record series, 1. Nottingham: University of Nottingham Centre for Local History, 1979.

Oxfordshire

HAVINDEN, M.A., ed. *Household and farm inventories in Oxfordshire, 1550-1590.* Oxfordshire Record Society, 44. 1965. Also published as Historical Manuscripts Commission joint publication, 10.

BRINKWORTH, E.R.C., & GIBSON, J.S.W., eds. *Banbury wills and inventories, part one: 1591-1620.* Banbury Historical Society, 13. 1985.

Shropshire

TRINDER, BARRIE, & COX, NANCY, eds. *Miners & mariners of the Severn Gorge: probate inventories for Benthall, Broseley, Little Wenlock, and Madeley, 1660-1764.* Chichester: Phillimore, 2000.

TRINDER, BARRIE, & COX, JEFF, eds. *Yeomen and colliers in Telford: probate inventories for Dawley, Lilleshall, Wellington and Wrockwardine, 1660-1750.* Chichester: Phillimore & Co., 1980.

Suffolk

ALLEN, MARION, ed. *Wills of the Archdeaconry of Suffolk, 1620-1624.* Suffolk Records Society, **31.** 1989.

EVANS, NESTA, ed. *The wills of the Archdeaconry of Sudbury 1630-1635.* Suffolk Records Society, **29.** 1987.

Warwickshire

HOLT, RICHARD, INGRAM, JANET, & JARMAN, JOHN. *Birmingham wills and inventories, 1551-1600.* Birmingham: University of Birmingham Dept. of Extra-mural Studies, 1985.

UPTON, ANTHONY A., ed. *Foleshill probate wills and inventories, 1535-1599.* Foleshill pamphlets, **4.** Lighthorne: the author, 1993.

ALCOCK, N.W. *People at home: living in a Warwickshire village, 1500-1800.* Chichester: Phillimore, 1993. Includes inventories for Stoneleigh.

Stratford-upon-Avon inventories I. 1538-1625: glossary. Publications of the Dugdale Society, **29,** [supplement]. 2002. This is a temporary publication; the full glossary will be published in a forthcoming Dugdale Society volume.

Worcestershire

WANKLYN, MALCOLM, ed. *Inventories of Worcestershire landed gentry, 1537-1786.* Worcestershire Historical Society, new series, **16.** 1998.

ROPER, JOHN S., ed. *Dudley probate inventories, 1544-1603.* Dudley: [J.S.Roper], 1965-6.

DYER, A. D., ed. 'Probate inventories of Worcester tradesmen, 1545-1614', in *Miscellanea II.* Worcestershire Historical Society, new series, **5.** 1967, 1-67.

Yorkshire

NEEDHAM, SUE. *A glossary for East Yorkshire and North Lincolnshire probate inventories.* Studies in regional and local history, **3.** Hull: University of Hull Dept. of Adult Education, 1984.

BREARS, PETER C. D., ed. *Yorkshire probate inventories, 1542-1689.* Yorkshire Archaeological Society record series, **134.** 1972.

THWAITE, HARTLEY, ed. *Abstracts of Abbotside wills 1552-1688.* Yorkshire Archaeological Society record series, **130.** 1968.

KIRK, G. E., ed. 'Some documents of Barnoldswick manor court of probate', in WHITING, C. E., ed. *Miscellanea vol. VI.* Yorkshire Archaeological Society record series, **118.** 1953, 53-84.

BERRY, ELIZABETH K., ed. *Swaledale wills and inventories 1522-1600.* Yorkshire Archaeological Society record series, **152.** 1998.

Chapman County Codes

The codes listed below have been used to indicate the counties in which particular words have been found in probate records. They have been used sparingly, and are provided merely as suggestions that the words concerned may be confined to a particular county or region. Such suggestions are not to be regarded as authoritative. Only the codes for pre-1974 English counties are listed here.

BDF	Bedfordshire	LND	London
BKM	Buckinghamshire	MDX	Middlesex
BRK	Berkshire	MON	Monmouthshire
CAM	Cambridgeshire	NBL	Northumberland
CHS	Cheshire	NFK	Norfolk
CON	Cornwall	NTH	Northamptonshire
CUL	Cumberland	NTT	Nottinghamshire
DBY	Derbyshire	OXF	Oxfordshire
DEV	Devon	RUT	Rutland
DOR	Dorset	SAL	Shropshire
DUR	Durham	SFK	Suffolk
ESS	Essex	SOM	Somerset
GLS	Gloucestershire	SRY	Surrey
HAM	Hampshire	SSX	Sussex
HEF	Herefordshire	STS	Staffordshire
HRT	Hertfordshire	WAR	Warwickshire
HUN	Huntingdonshire	WES	Westmorland
KEN	Kent	WIL	Wiltshire
LAN	Lancashire	WOR	Worcestershire
LEI	Leicestershire	YKS	Yorkshire
LIN	Lincolnshire		

Glossary

Abb Short-stapled wool of a particular quality, usually from the belly of the fleece.

Acacia Juice of the acacia tree, used as a drug.

Accates Victuals, purchased provisions. (Dby)

Accompt Account

Advowry Protector or patron, especially a patron saint, an advocate in heaven.

Adze Tool similar to an axe, with the blade at right angles to the handle, for straightening and smoothing wood surfaces; particularly used by *coopers.

Agistment The feeding of animals in a park, forest, or other pasture, for a stipulated price.

Aglets Metal decorations used at the end of laces to prevent them fraying; metal toys or spangles used for fastening garments together, e.g. the sleeves. Also used for the laces themselves.

Agnus Dei A cake of wax stamped with the figure of the Lamb of God, bearing a cross or flag, perhaps blessed by the Pope.

Alb A priest's white vestment or tunic, reaching to the feet.

Alchemy Any metal that imitates gold, e.g. brass.

Alcuin Antimony (Sal)

Ale Stool Stand for a cask of ale.

Alegar Sour ale; malt vinegar.

Alembic *Limbeck.

Alexanders An umbelliferous plant.

Algars *Hangings (1). (War)

Alias An alternative or assumed name.

Alkanet A red dye obtained from the roots of the anchusa.

Allamode, Allmood A thin, light, glossy black silk. (Lin)

Almain Rivets Light armour, made flexible by overlapping plates on sliding rivets. First used in Germany, i.e. aleman in Old French.

Almorie *Aumbry.

Aloe Bitter tasting purgative drug made from the juice of plants of the genus Aloe.

Altarage The revenue arising from *oblations at an altar.

Althæ Syrup A syrup obtained from the marsh mallow plant, used medicinally.

Alum Potassium aluminium sulphate, used as a mordant in preparing cloth for dyeing, and also in tanning; also used for curing bacon and sizing paper.

Alum Stone Stone trough for steeping skins in alum.

Amice White square of linen worn around the head and neck by priests when celebrating mass.

Amortize To alienate in *mortmain, i.e. to convey property to a corporation (usually ecclesiastical) in perpetuity.

Ancress Anchoress: a female hermit or nun.

Andier Dog *Andiron (1).

Andiron
1. A horizontal iron bar, supported by a short foot at one end, and an upright pillar or support, usually ornamental, at the other. A pair of these were placed at either side of the hearth, to support burning logs. The uprights may also have hooks for pots *etc.*, to hang above the fire, or may support a spit.
2. A pair of moveable iron plates to contract the fire grate.

Angel, Angel Noble Gold coin, introduced in 1465, portraying the Archangel Michael standing on and spearing the dragon; worth between 6s. 8d. and 10/-. Last coined by Charles I. This coin was presented to those touched for the 'King's evil'.

Angel, Angelica Water Perfume made from the herb angelica.

Anker
1. A measure of wine and spirits, varying by locality, but about four gallons in Dorset; a cask of that capacity.
2. Anchor.

Anoil To anoint with oil, give extreme unction to the dying.

Antic Grotesque, fantastic, or incongruous.

Antiphonary Book containing a collection of antiphons, i.e. short sentences sung alternately by different singers.

Apern Apron.

Apery, Aperyware *Napery.

Apothecary Druggist.

Apparel, Appill Personal clothing.

Apparitor The servant, attendant, or official messenger of a civil or ecclesiastical court.

Apple Iron, Roaster Iron implement for roasting apples over an open fire.

Apple Mill *Cider Mill.

Apple Wring Press for crushing apples to make cider. (Dev)

Appraiser The valuer / compiler of a probate inventory.

Appurtenance Minor right or property belonging to some other property, and passing with it.

Aqua Fortis *Strong Waters.

Aqua Vitae Alcoholic spirits, e.g. brandy, whisky; from the Latin for 'water of life'.

Archil A species of lichen, from which is produced a violet dye, giving a blue wash for walls.

Arders Ploughing and manuring; the state of being ploughed and manured; the value of land ploughed up.

Arfarrian *Orpharion.

Argil
1. Clay, especially potter's clay.
2. *Alum.

Argol Crude bitartrate of potassium, deposited by fermented wine on the sides of barrels as a hard crust, which becomes cream of tartar when purified.

Ark Wooden or metal box, chest or bin, with a domed lid, for flour, fruit, corn, *etc.*, suspended from the middle of the roof away from vermin.

Arming A term applied to anything armoured, or that is part of a soldiers equipment, e.g. arming coat, arming sword.

Armory *Aumbry.

Arquebus Portable gun, longer and larger than a musket, with a rest fastened to the barrel in order to support its weight when being fired.

Arras A rich tapestry, in which figures and scenes are woven in colour; a hanging screen of this material. Originally from the town in Artois, France.

Arrearages Arrears; payments overdue; debts.

Arrish Rake Rake for the stubble.

Arrow Timber Wood for making arrows.

Artificer Craftsman.

Asafoetida Resinous gum used as a flavouring in cookery, or medicinally.

Ash Balls Wood ash bound together with oil, which could be used as soap because of its potassium content.

Ash Baukes Beams made from ash trees.

Auger Carpenter's tool for boring holes in wood. It has a screw point and a handle at the top of the shaft by which it is screwed into the wood.

Aumbry Wooden cupboard for keeping victuals (usually prepared food rather than stores), with openings for air to circulate, perhaps using *hair cloth as sides to allow circulation. May also be used to store clothes, linen, etc. or, in a church, books, vestments, vessels, etc.

Awl Tool for piercing small holes in wood.

Axle Tree The fixed wooden beam on the ends of which the wheels of a cart or waggon, etc., revolve; an axle.

Ayes A harrow. (Gls)

B

Back
1. *Back Iron.
2. Chair back.

Back Band Broad leather strap or iron chain, passing over a cart saddle and supporting the shafts of a vehicle.

Back Board
1. Board used for the back of anything, e.g. a mirror.
2. A wooden screen to exclude draughts.
3. A scored wooden board for making oatcakes or rolling dough. (Ntt; Yks)

Back Board Chair Chair with a solid back which could be converted into a table.

Back Crook Iron hook hanging in the back of the hearth.

Back End Out house; perhaps a battery. (Lin; Yks)

Back House
1. Out-house or lean-to used as a kitchen, scullery, wash-house, etc.
2. *Bakehouse.

Back Hud, Plate Iron fire back, usually with raised ornamentation. (Dby)

Back Iron
1. Fire-back, often ornamental, placed against the masonry of the chimney.
2. *Back stone.

Back Pan Baking Pan.

Back Piece *Back Iron.

Back Side The rear part of a property; the back yard or farm yard, perhaps with outbuildings.

Back, Baking Spittle Flat wooden shovel or board used to place cakes, especially oatcakes, in the oven. (Yks, Lan)

Back Stone Flat plate of iron or stone (especially slate) on which oatcakes etc., were baked in an oven. It usually had a handle over the top.

Back Stool Hard chair with a back but no arms.

Back Sword Sword with only one cutting edge.

Backing Stock, Backitt Fire back.

Bacon Frame Rack for curing bacon, or hanging cured bacon, in the house. (Sts)

Bag A dry measure of quantity or weight, varying by locality, and by the nature of the goods concerned.

Bagging Bill *Bill(1) for reaping peas, beans, corn, *etc.*

Bail, Bale Hoop-handle of a kettle or similar vessel.

Bailiwick Area of a bailiff's jurisdiction.

Baize, Bays Originally a fine, light material introduced into England by Huguenot refugees in the sixteenth century; subsequently a coarse woollen cloth with a raised nap, made with a worsted warp and woollen weft, and used for curtains, coverings, *etc.*

Bake House Building or room with an oven for baking.

Baker Weight Measure used for assessing the quantity of flour milled from a given quantity of grain.

Balance
1. *Valance.
2. Scales, often described as 'a pair of'.

Balance Clock Clock controlled by a rotating balance wheel.

Bald
1. Piebald; animal having a white streak on the face.
2. Barren.

Bales, Balls, Ballowes Bellows.

Balet Small bale.

Balk
1. *Beam(1) of a balance.
2. Roughly squared beam of wood.

Ballys Small rod. (Gls)

Balm Water Medicinal preparation made from herbs.

Band
1. *Wearing band.

2. Metal hoop on a wheel rim.
3. *Bond.
4. Hinges with long flat bands of iron fixed to the back of a door.
5. Pair of strips of thin white material worn by men, around the neck, with the ends hanging down in front.

Band String Tasselled tie for fastening *bands.

Bandoleer A leather shoulder belt to support a musket and carry cases containing cartridges or charges.

Bandore A stringed musical instrument, resembling a guitar or lute and originating in Italy (where it was called a 'pandora'). It was used as a bass to accompany a *cithern.

Bangle Large rough stick, the cut branch of a tree. (War)

Bank Bench or long seat.

Banker
1. Cloth used to cover a seat or bench; a cushion for a form. Various fabrics might be used.
2. A long wooden work-bench, used in bricklaying or by masons.

Banyan Informal indoor gentleman's gown made of Indian cottons.

Bar Bar of iron at the base of the chimney, from which pots could be suspended.

Bare Used of a wain or cart without sides or covering, as opposed to *bound. (Dby, Ntt)

Bare Leap Large open basket, carried by two men, for removing chaff from a barn. (Dby)

Barefoot Wheel Wheel without an iron rim.

Bark
1. A small ship.
2. Candle box, formerly made of bark.
3. Bark used in tanning and dyeing.

Bark Bing Tool for beating bark in tanning.

Barkham, Barquam Pad on a horse's collar taking the pressure of the wooden or metal harness; a flat piece of leather protecting the horse's neck from rain. (Dby, Yks)

Bark House Tanning house; place where bark is stored.

Bark Tub Tub for storing bark, used in tanning.

Barley Mow Rick or stack of barley.

Barley Roll
1. Wooden cylinder pressed down and rolled across a heap of barley to separate the grain from the awns. (Gls)
2. A cart. (Bkm)

Barlines *Traces. (Ess)

Barm The foamy yeast which forms on fermenting malt liquor, used to leaven bread.

Barm Tub Tub used for fermentation in brewing.

Barm Skin A leather apron.

Barnacle A device inserted into a horse's nose by the blacksmith to keep it quiet whilst being shod.

Barnstaple Oven Ovens manufactured from local grit in the Barnstaple area; once heated by wood or furze fires, the grit retained sufficient heat to bake the bread or meat placed inside it when the ashes were removed.

Barras Coarse linen fabric originally imported from the Low Countries.

Barrateen A woven fabric.

Barrel Vessel smaller than a *hogshead in which liquids could be stored.

Barrey Hand barrow. (Dur)

Barrow Hog, Pig Castrated boar.

Barton Farmyard, or enclosed area of ground used for a specific agricultural purpose, e.g. a rick barton.

Bartree Wooden frame for the warp.

Base Court Court or yard at the back of a house, or perhaps in a castle or mansion, with its out-buildings; often occupied by servants.

Baselard Type of dagger usually worn at the *girdle.

Base(s)
1. Trestles.
2. Plaited skirt of cloth, velvet, or rich brocade, appended to a *doublet, and reaching from the waist to the knees.
3. The hangings of a bed, especially those which hang to the floor at the sides and feet.

Basils, Bassell Skins Sheepskins tanned in *bark, used especially in book-binding.

Basin Used for washing hands during the meal (knives and forks were not used).

Bason
1. Bench with a plate of iron, or a stone flag set in it, and a fire underneath, on which the first part of the felting process in hatting was performed.
2. *Basin.

Bass, Bast Plaited rush or straw used for matting. (Lin, Yks)

Bass Chair Rush-seated chair, often with sides and back made of straw coils in a wooden frame.

Bastard Of poor quality.

Bastet Sack or rough plaited basket to contain wool (Nfk).

Bath Stove A hot grate with an iron plate above the fire.

Battery Metalwork wrought by hammering.

Battledore
1. Leaf of paper mounted on a tablet of wood, with a handle and protective translucent horn, containing the alphabet, and perhaps also numerals, the Lord's Prayer, and other basic reading matter.
2. Wooden utensil used for mangling or smoothing clothes after washing.

Baulk A small cupboard in the ceiling close to the fire, for drying and storing meat; roof timbers from which meat was hung. (Dby, Yks)

Bavin A bundle of brushwood, bound with one band or *withy branch only, rather than two, as in the case of a *faggot.

Bawdekin Rich brocade; originally woven with woof of silk and warp of gold.

Bawtree Measure A measure of lead, the market for which was at Bawtree. (Dby)

Bay
1. A reddish brown colour, generally used of horses.
2. The division of a house or barn.

Bay Oil An oil obtained from the berries of laurel or bay trees, in appearance like butter.

Bay Salt Coarse salt obtained by evaporating sea-water under the sun's heat.

Beads String of beads to keep count of prayers, often in 'pairs'; a rosary.

Beam
1. *Beam and weights.
2. The wooden cylinder or roller in a loom on which the warp is wound before weaving, or the roller onto which the cloth is wound as it is woven.
3. The principal timber of a plough, to which everything else is fixed.
4. A crescent shaped piece of iron, raised at one end, on which raw hides were scraped with a *beam knife.

Beam and Weights A pair of scales with the weights. The beam, strictly speaking, was the transverse bar of the scales, but the term was often applied to the whole scales.

Beam Knife A long, heavy, curved knife used by tanners to remove hair from skins.

Bear Case, as in *pillow bear.

Bearing Term applied to items that are suitable for carrying, e.g. baskets, buckets, tubs, etc.

Bearing Cloth, Mantle, Sheet A baby's christening robe, or cloth used in child-bearing.

Beat Turf pared off for burning.

Beating Block Block used by craftsmen such as coopers and glaziers for beating things into shape.

Beating Horse Frame for beating clothes on.

Beattrihers A beating axe, i.e. an implement used to break up sods for burning. (Con)

Beaupers Fabric used for flags.

Beaver Hat Superior felt hat made from beaver fur.

Bed
1. The mattress only, which might be stuffed with *flock, feathers, down, etc.
2. The body of a cart.

Bed Boards The wooden planks which form the base of the bed, laid across the *bed stock.

Bed Case Wooden bedstead, or a mattresss cover. (Gls)

Bed Couch Day bed. (Lin)

Bed Hilling *Hilling (1).

Bed Performed Bed fully set up, complete with mattress, etc.

Bed Staves *Bed boards.

Bed Stock The front and back of a bed, especially its posts, between which the *bed boards were laid. Sometimes referred to as 'pair'.

Bed Tick, Tye *Tick.

Beddered Woman Bedmaker, i.e. an upholsterer.

Bederoll List of those remembered in *obits - often benefactors of the church.

Bedstead The wooden framework of a bed.

Bee Cote, Skep, Stall Hive.

Beef in Powder Salted beef.

Beef Pyke *Fleshcrook.

Beer Stool Stand for a cask of beer. (Nfk; Sfk)

Beeregar Sour vinegar made from beer.

Beetle Heavy headed wooden hammer or mallet used to hammer stakes into the ground, ram wedges, beat or crush flax and hemp, *etc.,* and having various shapes, dependant on the task for which it was used.

Beetle Ring Iron ring used to strengthen the heads of a *beetle.

Beeyn Bee hive. (War)

Belfry Temporary shed or rick-stand made of materials such as straw, furze, sticks, or wood, used as a shelter for animals, agricultural implements, beasts, *etc.* (Lin)

Bell Glass A bell-shaped glass frame or cloche, used for forcing plant-growth in the spring.

Bell Metal An alloy of copper and tin, or sometimes zinc and lead, used for casting bells and some domestic wares.

Bellises, Billowe Bellows.

Bellow Boards Wooden sides of a bellows.

Belly Band Band which passes around the body of a horse to check the play of the shafts.

Belting Hurdle Hurdle used to shalter animals. (War)

Bench, Bench Board Long form with a wooden backrest; the frame of the bench may be mentioned separately from the 'board', i.e. the seat. Sometimes fixed to the wall.

Bench Cloth Cushion or cloth for a *bench.

Bend The belting for the wheels of mill machinery. (Sts)

Bend Leather Thick leather used for soles of boots and shoes; the stoutest type of leather.

Bend of Leather Half an oxhide, with the thinner parts cut off.

Bender A mechanical device for setting or drawing cross-bows.

Bene Bees. (Chs)

Benjamin An aromatic gum used for perfuming gloves.

Bents Rushes or reeds.

Besom A brush made from twigs of broom, heather, birch, *etc.,* tied together around a handle; a broom.

Bibb Small tankard. (Gls)

Bice A dull azure colour.

Bickern, Bickhorn Small anvil, with two tapering ends.

Bidet Vessell on a low narrow stand, which can be bestriden when taking a bath.

Bigg Poor quality barley, coarse but hardy, which grows quickly on poor soils; used for malting.

Biggen Child's cap; nightcap. (Dor; Ham)

Biliment, Biliment Lace Ornament worn by a woman on her head or neck; ornamental lace.

Bill
1. An infantry weapon of various forms, ranging from a concave blade on a long handle, to an axe with with a spike on its back and the shaft ending in a spearhead; a *halberd.
2. A tool used in hedging, copse clearing, *etc;* a crescent-shaped blade often with a sharp hook. Its form varied greatly from place to place, and depended also on its specific purpose.
3. A chisel for cutting grooves in mill-stones. (Ess)
4. *Bill Obligatory.

Bill Obligatory A written statement acknowledging a debt and promising to pay it at a specified date.

Billet
1. Thick firewood.
2. Stick used as a weapon.
3. Small bar of metal.

Binding Braid, banding or fastening; cloth that secures the raw edges of a piece of fabric.

Bing
1. *Bark bing.
2. A bin or box for corn or flour.
3. A manger. (Sal)

Bing Stone The stone on which bark was beaten. (Dby)

Bink Wooden shelf or frame of shelves for storing earthenware or pewter; a plate rack or dresser. (Northern)

Bird Bolt A short, thick arrow, with a flat end, used to kill birds without piercing them.

Bird Broach, Spit Small spit for cooking poultry or game birds.

Bird Work Embroidery depicting birds.

Birding Piece *Fowling piece or shot-gun.

Birds Eye Rectangular ornamentation on fabric.

Bit Bridle Mouth-piece of a bridle.

Black Cup Leather drinking vessel, coated with tar or pitch. (Dby)

Black Jack
1. Large leather beer jug, coated with tar.
2. Zinc sulphide; a mining term.

Black Work
1. Type of embroidery done in black silk on linen.
2. In mining, any dark-coloured stratum.

Blades Shafts of a cart or wain.

Blank Table A plain, scrubbed, kitchen table.

Blend Corn Mixture of wheat and rye sown together.

Blinds Blinkers on a horse harness.

Blocks Sections of a mould used for shaping hats. The mould consisted of several variously shaped blocks which could be put together to form different shapes.

Blood Iron *Fleam.

Bluet A bluish woollen cloth.

Blunderbuss Flintlock gun with a wide bore, capable of firing many pellets; for short-range use.

Boar Frank Enclosure for boars; pigsty.

Board Timber plank forming the top of a table. Trestles are itemised separately. May also be a plank for other purposes, depending on the context, e.g. for a market stall.

Board Carpet *Board cloth.

Board Chair Chair for sitting at table.

Board Cloth Table cloth.

Board Shave Carpenter's plane.

Board with a Frame *Framed Table.

Boarded Made of boards nailed or pinned together, rather than jointed.

Boarded Bedstead *Bedstead with panelled or *wainscot head-board and/or foot.

Bob Wig Wig with curls turned up into 'bobs' at the bottom.

Bobbin Lace Lace made on a pillow with bobbins.

Bodge Measure of oats; half a peck.

Bodice Linen garment for the upper part of a women's body, strengthened with whalebone; also that part of a woman's dress above the waist, made separately from the *kirtle(1), but attached to it.

Bodkin
1. A bar forming part of the tackle for a plough or harrow. (Dor)
2. Long hair-pin used by women. (Lan)
3. Small pointed instrument of bone, iron or steel for making holes in cloth.

Body Girt Belly band of a saddle; *Girse (1).

Boiling Iron *Brandreth.

Bole Armeniac Pale, reddish earth from Armenia, used medicinally, and also as a constituent in gold size and canvas priming.

Bolling Lace Bobbled lace. (Dur)

Bolster
1. A long stuffed pillow on which the head is rested whilst in bed.
2. The block or plate on which metal to be punched is laid.

3. The solid lump of steel or other material between the tang and the blade of a wheelwrights knife.

Bolt
1. A bundle of reeds or straw, of a specific weight or size.
2. A roll of woven fabric, generally of a definite length.
3. An arrow for use with a cross-bow; generally short and stout.
4. A flour sieve, a sifter.

Bolting Sifting or sieving corn: the process of separating the flour from the husk.

Bolting Cloth Fine cloth used for *bolting.

Bolting House Room where flour is sifted and bread made.

Bolting Hutch, Mill, Tub, Tun, Which Tub or bin into which grain is sifted from the husks, or flour from the bran.

Bombasine Twilled or corded worsted material; cotton or silk was sometimes added. In black, the material was much used for mourning clothes.

Bond Promissory note or deed under which money was lent, or administrators and executors were required to perform their legal functions. It included a penalty for failure to comply with its conditions.

Bone Lace Made from linen thread, with bone bobbins.

Boose, Bowse Cattle stall. (Lin; Yks)

Boose Stake Wooden post where cows were tied in the cow house. (Dby)

Boot Hose Mens' over-stockings, worn inside boots to prevent the under-hose becoming soiled by the boot leather.

Boot Jack Contrivance for pulling boots off.

Boot Tree A foot-shaped piece of wood inserted into a boot or shoe to keep it in shape.

Borax A type of salt used in dyeing.

Borwte Hammer *Boute.

Boskin Wooden partition in a cow-house, with a ring for tying up cattle. (Dby)

Boss
1. A plasterers hod or tray.
2. A seat of straw.

Botham Skein or ball of thread or yarn. (Sts)

Bothies
1. A store house or shop. (Dby)
2. A water course. (Dby)

Bottle
1. A small container for carrying liquor probably made of leather.
2. A round moulding. (Oxf)
3. A bundle, especially firewood or hay.

Bouch, Bouk, Bowk Bucket; wooden pail with an upright handle.

Boule Type of handle. (Lin)

Boulter A long fishing line with many hooks.

Bound Used of a *wain or cart with sides, and perhaps a covering, as opposed to *bare. (Northern)

Bound Wheel Wheel with iron rim.

Boure Bower: a chamber.

Boute Blacksmiths heavy, two-handed hammer.

Bow
1. *Ox Bow.
2. *Bow Hurdle.
3. The semi-circular handle of a pail.
4. A stall for cattle. (War)
5. A high fire-guard. (Oxf)
6. Part of a *tumbrel. (War)

Bow Chair Chair with a bow-shaped back.

Bow Dye Scarlet dye from the dye-house at Bow, in East London.

Bow Hurdle A six-foot pole with projecting ends, over which a string of catgut (a 'bow') was drawn; the material from which hats were made was stretched on this. (Gls; Oxf)

Bow Saw Saw with a narrow blade set in a strong frame.

Bow Stave The wooden part of a bow for shooting arrows.

Bow String String for an archery bow, or for a hatter's bow.

Bowbarde *Cupboard. (Ham)

Box Wood of the box tree.

Box Iron A hollow, triangular-shaped iron, in which hot coals could be placed, for smoothing clothes.

Brach Pan *Dripping Pan. (Gls)

Bracken Ashes Ash from bracken was rolled into balls and used to make *lye (in place of soap).

Braid, Bread Board for pressing curd in cheese-making. (Sfk)

Brake
1. *Bread Brake.
2. A toothed instrument for breaking flax or hemp.
3. A heavy *harrow for breaking clods in rough ground.
4. A snaffle or bridle for a horse.
5. A framework intended to hold something steady, e.g. a horse's foot when being shod, a strainer placed over a tub.
6. A cart without a body, used in breaking horses. (Oxf)
7. A large barrow. (Oxf)
8. A hook or sickle for up-rooting grass. (Gls)

Brake Board *Bread Brake (2).

Brake Stool Stand on which hemp was placed to be crushed.

Branched Stuff, Branchis Textiles or fabrics with raised patterns.

Branches, Branch Candle Chandeliers, often made of brass, with a number of arms or branches.

Brand Iron
1. Branding iron, used for burning marks of ownership in livestock.
2. *Brandred (1).

Branded Heifer Heifer with burnt-on mark of ownership.

Branded Wheat Wheat affected by a fungoid disease, which makes it appear burnt.

Brandred, Brandreth, Brandize
1. *Gridiron or *trivet used to support cooking vessells over an open fire.
2. A wooden framework to support, e.g., barrels, hay stacks, *etc.*
3. A rail or fence surrounding a well.

Brank Buckwheat.

Brasen, Brason Made of brass. Brass pots were stronger than *latten; they were also better than iron, as they could be repaired.

Brass Faces Ornamentation on *andirons.

Brass Pieces Counters for a *shuffleboard.

Brawn A fattened boar.

Bray
1. Tool used in breaking hemp.
2. Horse bit.
3. Small piece of charcoal used in refining iron. (Wor)

Braying Stone Used like a pestle for pounding in a mortar.

Brazil
1. Scarlet dye from a redwood tree of the East Indies, and also of a South American species (from which the country is named); also, material dyed with it.
2. Brazil nut.

Brazil Pepper Brazil nut.

Breach Field A field newly ploughed from fallow, ready for sowing.

Bread Brake, Fleake
1. Slatted wooden box or hurdle suspended from the ceiling for storing bread.
2. A kneading trough.

Bread Grate *Bread brake (1).

Break Horn *Bickern.

Breast Plate Harness strap running across a horse's breast.

22

Brede Piece of material of the full width. (Dur)

Breeches Short trousers fastened beneath the knee, covering the loins and thigh.

Breeder Animal capable of breeding; often in-calf cows.

Breviary Book containing the daily offices, for use of clergy.

Brew House Room or out-house set aside for brewing.

Brewing Gutts A pipe or sink for liquid to flow out.

Brewing Keive *Keive

Bribe Piece cut off an end of cloth, which is damaged or imperfect; a short length of cloth. (Yks)

Bridges Satin *Bruges.

Bridgwater Woollen cloth originally from Bridgwater, Somerset.

Brigandine Body armour consisting of iron rings or small plates, sewed on canvas, linen or leather, and covered by similar material; originally in two halves, hence a 'pair of ...'. Worn by foot soldiers.

Brigg
1. Iron frame, often hinged, supporting pots and pans over the hearth. (Yks)
2. Wooden frame to support a *sile when draining curds in cheese-making, or the *temps when separating the malt from the *wort in brewing.

Briggs *Brogues

Brimstone Sulphur, used medicinally.

Brindle, Brinded Tawny brown, marked with streaks of a different hue.

Bristol Shot Lead shot made in Bristol.

Broach
1. Spit for roasting.
2. A chisel.
3. A piercing instrument.

Broad Cloth, Broads Fine, plain, black, hard-wearing cloth, weaved two yards wide with a short nap, used for men's outer clothing.

Broad Loom Loom (2) for *Broad cloth.

Broad Gold, Piece Gold coins struck by hammer, superseded after 1663 by the guinea, although legal tender until 1733; worth 20/-. They were much broader and thinner than the new coinage.

Broad Silk A wide piece of silk, as opposed to a ribbon.

Broad Weaver Weaver of *broadcloth.

Brocatelle Fabric similar to brocade, of silk or wool, used for tapestry, upholstery, etc.

Brod Round-headed nail made by a blacksmith.

Brogues Leather breeches.

Broiling Iron, Plate
1. A support for a cooking pot; a *grid iron.
2. A type of Dutch oven.

Brok Bracket: a small shelf, usually ornamental, for the wall of a room.

Brome Variety of grass resembling oats.

Broom Hook Hook for clearing undergrowth, especially broom or gorse.

Brown Holland Unbleached *Holland cloth.

Browse Brushwood, furze, etc., for kindling fires.

Brush Hook *Bill for cutting brushwood.

Bruges A type of satin made in Bruges, Flanders.

Brushing Chamber Room for dressing or smoothing flax.

Brussels Carpet Carpet with a worsted warp brought to the surface in loops to make the pile. Originally made in Brussels.

Buck
1. Body of a cart or waggon, especially its front.
2. Buckwheat: coarse wheat for animal feed.

Buck Iron Grooved iron used for making horse-shoes. (Gls)

Bucking The process of steeping clothes in *lye to cleanse them, when soap was rare and expensive. After steeping, the clothes were beaten with flat wooden bats; also applied to the clothes themselves.

Bucking Basket Washing or clothes basket.

Bucking Cooler, Loom, Tub Tub used in the process of *bucking.

Buckler Small round shield for personal defence, strapped to the left arm, or carried by a handle at the back.

Buckling Chains Chains for the harness of horse or oxen.

Buckram Fine linen or cotton; subsequently coarse linen stiffened with paste or gum.

Bud Bull, bullock or heifer aged one to two years.

Budge Lambskin, with the wool dressed outside to resemble fur.

Budget
1. Milk can shaped to be carried on the back.
2. A workman's bag, pouch, or wallet, usually of leather, and perhaps carried on horse-back.

Budget Kettle Small portable flask or billy-can.

Buff Coat Soldier's coat of stout leather dressed with oil, which provided some protection against weapons such as swords.

Buffet An early form of sideboard, with three shelves, some or all of which were open to display pewter *etc.*

Buffet Stool Low stool with an upholstered seat, set on a frame for use at table; a footstool.

Buffin Coarse cloth used for gowns; a garment made of this material.

Bugle Tube-shaped glass bead, usualy black, worn as jewellery.

Bulchin Bull calf.

Bulk Framework projecting from the front of a shop or stall.

Bullaines, Bullions
1. Bullion.
2. Gold or silver lace or braid.
3. Hooks or studs for fastening garments.

Bullen Brass weights. (Oxf)

Bumble Woven bull rushes, used for seating, *etc.*

Bunching Block Wooden block on which hemp or flax was beaten with a *beetle. (Nfk; Sfk)

Burdit Cotton fabric.

Bunting Trough Trough used in the process of bunting, i.e., sieving bran from the wheaten flour after it has been ground.

Burgage A freehold property in a borough, a house held by burgage tenure.

Burgundy Pitch The resinous juice of the spruce fir, from Neufchatel (formerly in Burgundy).

Burling
1. Yearling bullock or heifer.
2. The process of rectifying faults in newly made cloth.

Burling Iron Clothier's iron for removing unevenness in cloth.

Burn Branding iron. (Dby)

Burnt China China that is painted after the initial decorations, and re-fired.

Burnt Silver Silver calcined for use as a drug or pigment.

Burrier Tool for picking and *burling woollen cloth. (Dev)

Burthen
1. A load; the carrying capacity of a ship.

Bushel
1. A dry measure of capacity used for corn, *etc.,* varying in quantity according to locality, but generally equal to four pecks or eight gallons; a vessel holding this amount.
2. The iron rim of a wheel, which prevents it from wearing. (Dur)

Busk A strip of wood or whale-bone used in a woman's stays or corsets to stiffen and support them.

Buskin A light leather or cloth covering for the feet and lower legs; a half-boot or leather gaiters.

Buss
1. A young calf.
2. Wooden frame at the top of a wall. (Oxf)

Bustian A cotton fabric used for waistcoats, sometimes described as a coarse type of *fustian, sometimes distinct from it.

Bustimes A cotton fabric. (Con)

Butt
1. A cask for wine or ale, its capacity varying between 108 and 140 gallons.
2. The thicker part of anything, especially hides and skins, or the end of anything.
3. A heavy two-wheeled cart, made to tip. (Dev)
4. A small piece of land in an open field, usually of irregular shape.
5. Basket for catching fish, especially salmon.
6. A bee-hive.

Butter
1. Small tub for washing butter.
2. *Bolting cloth.
3. Blacksmith's tool.

Buttery Store room for drink and food; a cool room as opposed to the kitchen.

Butt Maund Basket fitted with two lids used for carrying butter and eggs.

Buttress Tool used to pare horses' hooves before shoeing.

Byland Headland in an open field, usually unploughed, and perhaps used as a footpath between the strips. (Chs)

Byrne Hooks Large hooks suspended from pack saddles, for carrying additional burdens. (Dby)

C

Cab A dry measure of capacity.

Cabinet Originally a box for valuables, but, by 1700, it had become a substantial piece of furniture with drawers concealed by doors which opened outwards.

Cabriole Leg of a table or other piece of furniture, curved outwards at the knee, and tapering inwards below, with an ornamental foot.

Cad The youngest and smallest animal; especially used of pigs.

Cadawe, Caddow A coarse woollen covering, made in Ireland, and used as a horse blanket or a bed covering.

Caddis
1. Material such as wool, cotton, *etc.,* used to pad clothes.
2. A worsted tape used for garters and *girdles.
3. A coarse, cheap serge.

Cade Young animal abandoned by its mother and fed by hand.

Cade Coals Coal for domestic use. (War)

Cader Cradle.

Cades Shreds of any material. (Wor)

Caffa Rich silk cloth similar to *damask.

Cake Print Baker's implement for making small cakes. (Dby; Sts)

Cake Sprittle Thin board for turning oat-cakes during cooking.

Calaber Fur from a foreign species of squirrel, perhaps originally imported from Calabria.

Calamanco A fine woollen satin-twilled stuff, checked or brocaded, and glossy on the surface, made in Flanders. Much used for waistcoats and *breeches in the 18th c.

Calash A light carriage with removeable folding hood and low wheels.

Calbot *Cobiron (1). (Sal)

Caldern *Cauldron

Calico A general name for light cotton cloths, originally plain, but later frequently printed with designs, and glazed, originally imported from India, but subsequently made in England.

Caliver A light musket or blunderbuss; the lightest fire-arm available apart from the *pistol, fired without a rest.

Caliver Flask Leather or metal case holding gunpowder.

Calkins The parts of a horse-shoe which are turned down and sharpened to prevent slipping.

Call
1. Dish shelf or rack. (Yks)
2. Close fitting cap for women.
3. Whistle.

Call of Gold Ornamental net-work.

Callis Sand A fine white sand, originally from Calais, used for blotting ink, and for scouring and cleaning pewter.

Cambrel Butcher's hook for hanging carcasses.

Cambric, Camerick A type of fine white linen, originally made at Cambrai, in France. The term was also applied to a hand-spun cotton imitation.

Came Grooved bars of lead which held the glass in lattice windows.

Camlet A fine, light linen made from a combination of wool, silk and hair, and especially from the wool of angora goats. It is said to have originally been made from camel hair in the Middle East, but this is uncertain. Frequently used for bed hangings, upholstery, and womens' clothing.

Camp Chair Folding chair.

Campernows Ale potage made with sugar and spice.

Can
1. A cylindrical vessel for holding liquid; a drinking vessel, not necessarily metal.
2. A bucket for milk or water.

Candle Case Case or box for candles.

Candle Branch
1. Socket to place a candle.
2. Chandelier.

Candle Mould Pewter or tin mould for making candles.

Candle Plate Metal plate with a pricket-type spike to take a candle, or a single socket on a round plate.

Cannell Bituminous, bright-burning coal that could be cut and polished like jet. Occasionally used for candlesticks and other small objects.

Cannequin A white cotton cloth from the East Indies.

Canopy *Hangings (2) suspended over a bed.

Canstick Candlestick, originally using a *pricket rather than a socket to hold the candle.

Cantch Small amount of unthreshed corn. (War)

Cantle Fragment or remnant.

Canterbury Stand to hold music portfolios.

Cantharides Dried beetle, used for medicinal purposes.

Cantoon A strong *fustian, with fine cording on one side, and a smooth bright finish on the other.

Canvas Coarse, unbleached cloth made from hemp or flax, used especially for window curtains and for supporting mattresses, and very popular for *doublets.

Cap Case
1. Travelling bag or wallet for personal belongings.
2. Box, chest or casket; a receptacle of any kind.

Cap Cloak Cloak with a hood.

Cap Paper
1. Wrapping paper.
2. A size of writing paper.

Cap Staff Capstan or crane.

Caple Horse. (Northern)

Caplin The strong leather loop or hinge on a flail.

Capon Castrated cock being fattened for the table.

Caponet A small or young *capon.

Capouche A hood or cowl, especially that of Capuchin monks.

Car Four-wheeled vehicle. (War)

Car Slide A type of sledge.

Carbine A short, light musket, accurate in fire, but with a short range; used by cavalry.

Carchew, Carchowe, Carcheife *Kerchief

Card Iron toothed comb set in leather, used to part and comb out fibres of wool or flax in preparation for spinning, or to raise the nap on cloth. Used in pairs, one of which was a fixed *stock card, the other held in the hand.

Card Leaves The sheets of leather into which the teeth of *cards were inserted.

Card Table, Pair of Table used for playing cards, consisting of two boards hinged together which, when opened, formed a table. Often covered in cloth or *baize.

Cardinals Hat A flat, broad-rimmed dish. (Ham)

Carding Stock *Stock card.

Care Sunday The fifth Sunday in Lent, or the Sunday immediately preceding Good Friday; also referred to as Passion Sunday.

Carl Hemp The seed-bearing hemp plant, of stronger growth and coarser fibre than the male plant. 'Carl' means male, but the name was mistakenly given to the female plant. Used in rope-making.

Carlin A Neapolitan silver coin worth about four pence, or, later, two pence.

Carob Fruit or pod of a Levantine tree.

Carpet Heavily woven wool used as bed coverings or table cloths, etc. Not usually for the floor, except in the houses of the very wealthy.

Carpet Cushion Thin cushion for benches and seating.

Carr Marshy land, bog, or fen, perhaps with willows, alders, etc., growing on it.

Carral A play pen for children. (Lin)

Carrel, Carrey Mixed fabric of worsted and silk, or sometimes linen yarn.

Carriage A wheeled vehicle generally; most likely to refer to a cart rather than anything grander in most probate records.

Carsey *Kersey

Cart A two-wheeled farm vehicle, smaller than a *wain, without springs.

Cart Saddle Small saddle for a horse's back, to support the shafts.

Cart Staves Poles, rods, etc., used on carts to hold the load on.

Carthen *Cauldron.

Carthamus Bastard saffron, whose flowers yield red and yellow dyes.

Case
1. Wooden container for a chamber pot.
2. Chest of drawers.
3. *Bed case. (Gls)

Casement Frame forming a window, on hinges, attached to one of the uprights of the frame in which it is fixed.

Caser A coarse sieve. (Dur)

Cask A barrel of indeterminate size.

Cask Chair Chair made from a cask or barrel.

Caslin Inferior calf skin. (Sal)

Cassock A long loose coat or gown, worn by both sexes.

Cast Back Iron fire-back.

Caster
1. Best quality beaver fur; hats made of this, or of a rabbit skin imitation.
2. Small container with perforated top for sugar or pepper etc.

Caster Hat Hat made of beaver fur, or, later, rabbit-skin.

Castile Soap Fine, hard soap from Spain made with olive oil and soda.

Castilion A type of cloth.

Casting Net Fishing net that swept the bottom of the river.

Castling Calf born before the usual time.

Cathern, Cawthern *Cauldron.

Catshid A sawn plank. (Gls)

Cattle The word for goods, *'chattel', derived from the word 'cattle'. The number of cattle was the measure of a man's wealth, and hence the word changed its meaning to 'goods', as well as changing its pronunciation.

Caudle A warm drink: thin gruel mixed with wine or ale, sweetened and spiced, mainly for the sick and their visitors.

Caudle Cup Two-handled cup, perhaps with a lid, for drinking *posset or *caudle.

Caul Rope Rope made from coarse hemp. (Oxf)

Cauldron Large metal vessel with three legs for cooking, sometimes made of brass, standing over the fire, for stews, *etc.*

Caverings Chaff or corn husks used to fill a mattress. (Sfk)

Cawfoy *Kersey.

Ceiled *Sealed.

Ceiling *Sellyng.

Cellar A store-room for provisions; a granary, *buttery, or pantry, which could be above or below ground.

Cellaret Case or sideboard for storing wine bottles.

Cellot *Skillet. (Gls)

Celour
1. A canopy over a bed, or its hangings.
2. Wall tapestry or screen of drapery.

Cerce *Searce: a sieve or strainer.

Certum A garland. (Lin)

Cess
1. Toilet.
2. Tax, rate or fee.

Cettle
1. *Settle.
2. *Kettle (1).

Chafer A small, closed, transportable brazier containing burning charcoal or hot ash, on which a *chaffing dish was placed.

Chaff Bed Mattress filled with chaff and husks of corn.

Chafing Dish A dish to put on a *chafer, to keep food warm.

Chain Lace Braid lace, made from a single cord knotted upon itself.

Chain
1. A part of the harness attached to *butts, *ploughs, *trees and *yokes, *etc.*
2. Warp.

Chair Cart A light cart, a chaise, drawn by one horse.

Chair Chest A wooden chair with arms, usually panelled, with a seat on hinges which lifted to reveal storage space.

Chair Stool Chair with a back but no arms; stool with a back.

Chair Table Chair with a solid back which could be folded down on to its arms to form a table.

Chaise Light open carriage for travelling.

Chaise Mayrez Cart for transporting fresh fish. (Gls)

Chalder A dry measure, varying in quantity from 32 to 40 *bushels, for coal, lime, fish, *etc.*

Chaldron
1. *Cauldron.
2. *Chalder.

Chalk Line Cord rubbed with chalk, used to lay down a straight line on material as a guide for cutting.

28

Chamber Any room, excluding the hall or the kitchen, used for any purpose, but often an upstairs bedroom, and sometimes a parlour; a private room.

Cham(b)let *Camlet.

Champion Land in open fields divided into strips, as opposed to land held in *severalty.

Chandler
1. Candlestick; chandelier.
2. Candlestick maker or trader.

Changeable A fabric of changeable colour, either shot or variegated; often silk.

Chantry Endowment for a priest to say mass for souls of specified dead; often refers to the chapel or altar where such masses were said.

Chape Metal plate of a scabbard, especially that which covers the point; the scabbard itself.

Chapman An itinerant pedlar, hawker, or merchant; one who buys and sells; a trader.

Chare
1. *Plough Share.
2. Chair.

Charger A large flat dish for carrying a joint of meat to the table; the largest dish in a *garnish of *pewter.

Charing Rake Rake for separating the chaff from corn. (Dby)

Chariot An open *carriage; a cart or wagon.

Chased Ornamental with embossed work.

Chasuble A priest's vestment; a sleeveless *mantle worn over the *alb and stole when celebrating mass.

Chattel Moveable possessions, including livestock; also including leasehold property - but not other types of real estate. All chattels should have been listed in probate inventories. See *Cattle.

Chattel Lease A lease, which could be bequeathed by will. Sometimes referred to as chattels, chattel estates, or simply leases.

Chechyng, Chicthing Kitchen.

Cheeks Upright stones or irons in a fireplace; the sides of a grate.

Cheese Board, Bread Round board placed on top of a cheese to press it down.

Cheese Brig Wooden cross bars resting on the cream pan to support the skimming bowl so that it may drip into the liquid below.

Cheese Cowl Tub or pail in which cheese and rennet were mixed in the early stages of cheese-making.

Cheese Cratch, Heck, Racka, Vecke Rack for drying and storing newly made cheese.

Cheese Ladder Support for the cheese vat to rest upon over a cheese tub whilst the whey is pressed out.

Cheese Mote *Cheese Vat.

Cheese Press, Cheese Wring Press used in cheese-making, to compress the curds and expel the moisture and whey.

Cheese Vat Mould in which cheese was made. The curds are placed in it, and the cheese is shaped under a press, expelling the whey.

Chell, Chendel Candlestick.

Cherkey *Turkey.

Chest Bed *Press Bedstead.

Chested Placed in coffin.

Cheverell Kid leather, noted for its pliability and stretching capability.

Chewtawe *Hatchell. (Wor)

Cheyeer Mill A shear-mill: for making either plough shares or shears.

Cheyney
1. China.
2. A printed woollen or worsted fabric, sometimes used for curtains.

Chilver Ewe lamb.

Chimlin *Kimnel.

Chimney The term may refer to iron structures erected over open hearths, prior to the time when stone chimneys became common.

Chimney Board Board used to close a chimney during the summer.

Chimney Crane Iron implement fixed with brackets to the back of a hearth, which could be swung out to support cooking pots over the fire.

Chimney Glass Mirror hung on a chimney breast.

Chimney Money Hearth tax, imposed between 1662 and 1689.

Chimney Piece Hood over the fire to channel smoke into the chimney; usually ornamental, and often associated with a shelf or mantle.

Chin Cloth A band of cloth passing under a woman's chin; a muffler.

Chintz Painted or stained *calico imported from India, usually glazed.

Chirurgery Surgery.

Chittle *Kettle.

Chopping Block, Stock
1. A piece of tree-trunk on which wood was chopped up.
2. A block of wood on which food was chopped up.

Chrisom, Christening Sheet A white sheet or robe worn by babies and children at baptism; a token of innocence. If the child died within a month it was used as a shroud; otherwise it was given as an offering at the mother's churching or purification.

Church Work Fabric, possibly richly embroidered, which had belonged to a pre-Reformation church, but which had been sold off and put to secular use when the reformers arrived, perhaps cut up into cushions.

Churchys Kerchief.

Churn A conical shaped vessel with a perforated plunger worked by an up and down motion, used to make butter from cream. Replaced by the revolving churn, which was barrel-shaped, and revolved on pivots.

Churn Staff Wooden plunger or pale used to agitate cream in a churn in order to make butter.

Chusinett *Cushionet.

Cider Mill, Press, Wring Apples for cider were, in theory, first crushed in a cider mill, and then pressed in a cider press or wring to extract the juice. However, these terms were often used synonymously.

Cilhouse *Gyle House.

Cistern
1. Water container for the household, sometimes called a *lead (2) and frequently located in the kitchen.
2. Brewing vat.

Cithern, Citterne A musical instrument similar to a guitar, strung with wire, and played with a plectrum.

Cittermister *Kidderminster Stuff.

Cives *Keives.

Civet An animal ranking in size between a fox and a weasel; hence a 'purse of civet' is made from its fur.

Clam Clamp, vice, or pincers, sometimes used to hold leather together for sewing.

Clapboard, Clapholt Split oak used for wainscoting and barrel staves, *etc.,* or for weather boarding roofs and walls.

Clasper Metal fastener.

Clatts Cow dung used as fuel.

Clavichord A small keyboard instrument with a soft tone.

Clavel, Clavy Beam of wood serving as a lintel over the fire-place; the mantel.

Cleat Wedge-shaped piece of wood, especially as used in securing the moveable parts of ploughs and scythes.

Cleaver
1. Butcher's knife.
2. Large wooden wedge for splitting timber.

Clerk Clergyman.

Clevis
1. Strong hooks fixed to the end of a chain or rope.
2. U-shaped piece of iron bolted to the end of a plough or wain, forming a loop to which tackle might be attached.
3. Part of the tackle of lifting gear.

Clew A small measure of yarn, a ball.

Cliching Knife Knife for trimming horses' hooves.

Cloak Bag Travelling bag or portmanteau.

Cloam, Cloaming Earthenware. (Dev)

Clock Silk thread pattern on the side of stockings.

Clock Reel Wooden device to measure the length of a skein of yarn. (Nfk; Sfk)

Clog, Clodge Piece of wood attached to a beast to impede movement. (Dby)

Clog, Clodge Wheels Wooden cart wheels made out of planks, without spokes.

Close
1. An enclosed field.
2. Yard for cattle; farmyard.

Close Barrell, Chair, Jake, Stool Commode or chamber pot, generally consisting of a pan or pot enclosed in a box or barrel type structure, to keep the smell in.

Close Bed A box bed, totally enclosed and entered by sliding doors or shutters.

Close Bonk Bucket with a lid or cover used for washing.

Close Cart A farm cart.

Close Hose Close fitting hose.

Close Kit Wooden tub for washing clothes. (Dby)

Cloth Female Fine linen. (Lin)

Cloth of Tissue A rich cloth, often interwoven with silver or gold.

Cloth Press Press used in the process of cloth finishing.

Clothes Hussey Box for storing clothes. (Gls)

Clothier A maker and / or seller of cloth.

Clout
1. A metal patch or plate used by a blacksmith for mending, and especially one fixed to an *axle tree or to parts of a plough to prevent wear by chafing.
2. A fragment, a piece.
3. A piece of cloth containing pins and needles.

Clout Leather Thick leather for shoe soles or for patching.

Clove Bark The spice from a species of cinnamon tree, with the flavour of cloves.

Clove Iron *Clevis.

Clowes Thread wound on bobbins. (Lan)

Coal
1. Charcoal. This is likely to be the usual meaning as *sea coal was not suitable for cooking on an open hearth.
2. *Sea Coal.

Coal Rake For raking cinders from an oven when it was hot enough to bake bread.

Coal Tankard Coal scuttle. (Gls)

Coal Vat Vat used to measure coal.

Coarslett *Corselet.

Coast Barrel holding 9 gallons, or a measure of this amount. (Dev)

Coat
1. An outer garment.
2. Petticoat.

Cobbars Horse equipment. (Chs)

Cobard, Cobart, Cobberd
1. *Cupboard.
2. *Cobiron.

Cobiron
1. Bar with hooks which supported a spit over the hearth, used instead of *andirons (1). They rested at an angle at the back of the fireplace, with the spit placed on two hooks.
2. A cradle for firewood.

Coble Open fishing boat, without deck or keel, but with sharp bows and a flat, sloping stern.

Cobweb Lawn Very fine transparent linen fabric.

Cocer A dealer. (Lin)

Cochineal A brilliant red dye, made from the dried body of an insect, *coccus cacti;* also used medicinally.

Cock
1. Tap.
2. Small conical heap.
3. Ship's boat.

Cock and Chain Piece of iron with notches, fixed at the end of the plough beam.

Cockloft Space between the ceiling and the roof, reached by ladder; perhaps an attic or garret.

Cockshut Net Net suspended between two poles for catching woodcock in flight, perhaps at twilight.

Coconut A coconut shell cup, usually with a silver framework and lip.

Cod, Codware Pillow or cushion.

Codbear *Pillow Bere.

Coffer Lockable box or chest, often with a leather-covered lid, used for the storage of clothes or valuables.

Coffin Small chest or box.

Cog Type of fishing boat distinctive to the Rivers Humber and Ouse. (Lin; Yks)

Coif Close-fitting cap, covering the top, back and sides of the head, worn by women or clerics.

Colander Perforated metal vessel used as a sieve or strainer.

Collar Usually refers to the bridles or halters of horses and oxen.

College Cup An early form of *porringer.

Collock A wooden tub or pail.

Colt Horse less than five years old, but no longer a foal.

Colt Irons Used to bind the *coulter to the frame of the plough.

Comb
1. *Card.
2. A measure of capacity; four bushels.
3. A brewing vat or tub. (Bkm)

Comfit A sweetmeat made from fruit and sugar.

Commerce Table Table used to play a game called 'commerce', the 18th century equivalent of Monopoly.

Commode
1. Chest of drawers; it did not become a *close stool until the 19th century.
2. A tall head-dress of silk or lace, on a wire frame, worn by women.

Common Field Land owned in common by the whole community, usually divided into arable strips for individual farmers, who also had pasture rights over the whole field.

Commons Provender, provisions.

Comparcioner Joint owner; one who shares an inheritance or estate with another.

Compass Saw A saw with a narrow blade which cuts circularly.

Compass Compost: manure or night soil.

Compass Window Semi-circular bay window.

Compast Round.

Composition Money Payment made in lieu of a larger amount or other obligation; a sum paid by royalists to Parliament to 'compound' for their 'delinquency'; a *fine.

Compter *Counter; also the name of certain debtors' prisons.

Conduit Pipe or channel for running water.

Confection Medicinal preparation made from various drugs.

Cony Rabbit; rabbit skin.

Cony Hayes Rabbit warren.

Cony Flax Rabbit fur.

Cool Back Cooler, especially in a *brewhouse.

Cool House Room in which perishables are kept cool.

Cooler Shallow pan, staved tub or trough in which milk, *wort, or other liquids are set to cool.

Cooling Lead Large tub for brewing.

Coop
1. A basket, probably wicker.
2. Small shed or hutch for poultry or other animals
3. A cart with closed sides and ends, suitable for carting dung, lime, *etc.* Probably with two wheels or perhaps mounted on sled runners.

Cooper Maker of barrells and other wooden vessels made of staves and hoops.

Coopery Ware Collective term for tubs, barrel, *keives, casks, *etc.,* made of staves and hoops by a *cooper.

Cop
1. Cover for a wagon. (Sal)
2. The beam placed between a pair of draught oxen. (Dby)

Cope Priest's vestment, resembling a long cloak, made from a semi-circular piece of silk or other material, without sleeves.

Copper Large vessel made of copper, used for cooking or laundry purposes, or for brewing.

Copperas Type of salt, used in dyeing, tanning, and ink-making. Also known as green vitriol, or sulphates of iron and zinc.

Copse *Clevis (2).

Copsole Wedge for keeping the plough's *coulter at the right angle.

Copyhold Land held by copy of the manorial court roll, in accordance with the custom of the manor.

Corbut Deep tub for salting meat. (Dev)

Cord
1. Cords were attached to *bedframes and made to form a tight net or web to support a rush or straw *mat and the *bed, i.e. the mattress.
2. A measure of sawn wood.

Cord Wood Smaller branches cut in lengths of four feet or so and stacked in 'cords', for fuel and charcoal-making.

Cordovan Fine Spanish leather made from goatskins, originally from Cordova.

Cordwainer Leather worker, usually a shoe-maker; originally a worker in *cordovan.

Corf, Corve
1. A basket made of hazel-rods, in which coal was carried to the surface in mines; subsequently, a wagon used for the same purpose.
2. A measure of coal.

Coriander A plant whose seeds are used for flavouring purposes.

Corkell Grindstone. (War)

Cornish Mat Wall to wall rush mats to be found in the grandest rooms.

Corporal, Corporas Linen used during the celebration of the mass to stand the bread and wine on, and to cover it.

Corr Fish Salted fish. (Dev)

Corse Ribbon or band, ornamented with metal-work or embroidery, and used as a *girdle or garter.

Corse Present *Mortuary.

Corselet, Corslet A light iron breastplate worn by foot soldiers.

Corser A dealer, especially a horse dealer.

Corvisor *Cordwainer.

Coster Wall or bed *hangings (2).

Costrel Large bottle or wooden keg, which had ears or a handle, by which it could be suspended from the waist or neck, and carried to the field or on a journey.

Cote Small shed for pigs, sheep, hens, *etc.,* or for storage.

Cotter Small iron pin, key, or wedge for securing a bolt.

Cotterell Adjustable hook, crane, or bar, for hanging pots over a fire. (Southern)

Cotton A woollen cloth with a frizzy nap.

Couch, Couch Bed A day bed without canopy or hangings.

Couch Chair A backless sofa against a wall with an arm at each end; a long *settle (1).

Coucher Table cloth.

Couching Floor, House Floor or room where grain was spread to germinate in the preparation of malt or woad.

Coulett *Coverlet.

Coulter A plough's iron blade, fixed in front of the share, to cut the soil vertically; the share then cuts it horizontally.

Counter, Counter Board, Counter Table
1. Desk or writing table where accounts could be prepared, money counted, *etc.*
2. Dresser or side-table.

Counter Beam The bars from which the scales of a balance are suspended.

Counterfeit Dishes made of base metal, as opposed to silver.

Counterpane, Counterpoint A quilted *coverlet; the uppermost covering for a bed.

Counting House Room for keeping accounts, receiving moneys, *etc.*

Coup *Coop.

Couple A ewe and a lamb together.

Course Sails on the lower yards of a ship.

Court Cupboard Two or three tiered sideboard, perhaps with doors to the lower tier; pewter or plate could be displayed on top, linen stored below, perhaps with more pewter.

Court Leet Manor or hundred court, held twice yearly, concerned with minor misdemeanours, suits for debt, appointment of constables, *etc.*

Court Roll Record of the business of a manorial court, kept on a roll of paper or parchment, and including much information on tenurial matters.

Courtledge *Curtilage.

Covart *Coverlet.

Covenant An agreement between master and servant, for the latter to serve for a specified period in return for board, wages *etc.*

Covenant Year A year's work agreed between master and servant at the end of the latter's apprenticeship.

Coventry Blue, Coventry Thread Thread made in Coventry, usually blue, and used for embroidery.

Cover Fire Cover to put over a fire to keep it burning with safety overnight.

Covered Chair Chair with padded seat and back.

Coverings *Coverlet.

Coverlet The uppermost bed covering, which could be made of various materials; a quilt or *counterpane.

Covert *Coverlet.

Cowl
1. A large tub for water, usually with two ears, through which a cowl staff could be passed so that it could be carried by two men.
2. An open tub used for cooling in brewing or butter-making, or for salting meat.

Cow Rack Hay rack for cattle.

Coytte
1. *Coif.
2. Matted sheep's fleece used as a doormat. (Lin)

Crab Lock Crab-shaped locks with five points for locking soft material such as money bags.

Crab Mill, Press Mill or press for pounding or crushing crab apples in the making of cider or verjuice.

Crack, Crackle Implement for preparing hemp. (Dby; Sts)

Cracknel Hard, crisp biscuit.

Cradle
1. Framework of bars, rods, cords, *etc.,* for holding or protecting something.
2. A light wooden frame attached to a scythe, with a row of long curved teeth parallel to the blade, designed to ensure that the mown grass fell compactly into even swathes.

Cradle Cloth *Swaddle bands.

Cradle Iron A framework of bars, or a grating, supporting cooking pots beside a fire.

Crane An iron bar fixed on a pivot in the chimney, from which pots are suspended over a fire.

Crape A light cloth, thin worsted stuff, made in Norfolk, sometimes used for woollen shrouds, which were compulsory after 1678; also for the clothes of clergy.

Cratch
1. Storage rack or manger for animal fodder.
2. Framework from whcih *flitches were suspended.
3. *Handle Cratch.

Crate
1. A hurdle.
2. Box with open bars or slots.

Crates A pair of panniers used for carrying heavy goods on pack-horses. (Dby)

Crayer Small trading ship.

Creale, Creel Osier basket for carrying fish. (Lin; Yks)

Crease *Crest.

Creeper
1. Iron dogs placed between the *andirons in a grate, to support burning logs.
2. Small frying pan with three legs.

Cresset
1. Iron container holding pitched rope, grease, or oil, to be burnt as a light; mounted on a pole or hung from the roof.
2. Device for hanging pots over a fire.
3. Small pan for boiling lead. (Dby)

Crest, Crest Tile Tile for the ridge of a roof.

Crest, Crest Cloth Type of linen cloth.

Crewel
1. Thin worsted yarn for embroidery or tapestry.
2. Embroidery needles.
3. Embroidery worked in wool onto linen.

Crib
1. A barred rack containing fodder for cattle to feed from; a *cratch.
2. A baby's cradle.
3. The body of a cart.

Cricket A low foot-stool, three-legged, perhaps used when milking cows.

Crock
1. A metal pot generally of brass or iron, with three short legs and a handle from which it could be hung.
2. An earthenware pan.
3. *Crook.
4. Soot.

Crocus Saffron, used as a yellow dye; cloth dyed with saffron.

Croft Enclosure, usually adjacent to the dwelling house, and used for tillage or pasture.

Crok Hangings *Hangings (1).

Cromb Wooden handled rake with two long hooked prongs, used for spreading manure.

Crook A hook, which could be of various different kinds. A pair of crooks were often hung above the hearth to support cooking utensils. Crooks might be found associated with ploughs or used to hold loads on the backs of pack-horses. Not to be confused with *crocks, although frequently with the same spelling.

Cross
1. Cross-bow; a weapon with a bow fixed on a wooden stock, with a device for holding and releasing the string.
2. Coopers tool for cutting a groove at the end of a cask to fit the lid.

Cross Bridge The frame at the back of a wagon which hold the side pieces in place.

Cross Cloth
1. Linen cloth worn on the forehead.
2. Knitted handkerchief. (War)

Cross Staff Instrument for measuring the altitude of heavenly bodies.

Cross Week Rogation week.

Crow Bar of iron with one end slightly bent, used as a lever; a crow-bar.

Crown English coin worth five shillings; also the French 'ecu', often seen in England in the sixteenth century.

Crown Gold Gold of high quality.

Crown Lace Lace patterned with crowns, acorns and roses.

Crows Rotatable form of *Trippet.

Cruck Wooden pail for carrying water or milk.

Cruet Vessel to hold wine or holy water at the celebration of the eucharist, *etc.*

Crum Crooked.

Crupper Leather strap which passed from the saddle under the horse's tail, to prevent the saddle sliding forward.

Crusado Portuguese coin bearing the sign of the cross.

Cruse
1. Small glass bottle holding vinegar or oil, which could be poured out slowly through a narrow pipe on the side.
2. Small earthenware jar or pot, usually for drinking.

Crusk, Cruskin Wooden or earthenware drinking-cup; pot, jar or bottle. (Dby)

Crust, Crust Board Plank of timber from the side of a log, with bark on one side.

Cub
1. A *crib for fodder: a bin, pen or receptacle.
2. Cage or *coop(2) for poultry and other animals.
3. Young animal.

Culgee Figured Indian silk.

Culm Poor quality coal used in lime-burning and for drying malt.

Culter *Coulter.

Cumin An umbelliferous plant grown for its seed, used in cooking.

Cupboard Board, supported by legs, and perhaps with shelves, used to store and display crockery, and especially cups; a sideboard. Easily confused with variants of *cobiron.

Cupboard Table Side table with shelves to display silver or pewter.

Cup Drinking vessel, usually of pewter or tin.

Curb
1. Stand in a brewery to support a cask.
2. Framing round the top of a brewers' copper.
3. Two-handled windlass.
4. Framing around a well.

Curnock A measure of corn, usually four bushels of barley or oats, and three of wheat.

Curry Comb Metal instrument for grooming horses.

Currier
1. An early firearm.
2. A tradesman who dresses and colours leather after it has been tanned.

Currying Knife Knife used by a *currier to dress leather after tanning.

Curtain Likely to be for a *bedstead rather than a window; not used for the latter until the 18th c.

Curtal Horse with its tail docked.

Curtilage Small court or yard attached to a house or farm.

Cushion Stool Stool with a padded seat.

Cushionet A small cushion; a pin-cushion.

Cut Sweet new wine.

Cut Work Open-work lace or embroidery.

Cutling Tub Tub for coarse oatmeal.

Cuttleaxe Cutlass: a short sword with a wide, flat, slightly curved blade.

Cuttle Bone Shell of the cuttlefish, used in polishing.

Cutwith The cross-bar of a *plough or *harrow to which the *traces are attached.

Cyder Wring *Apple Wring

Cypress
1. Wood from the cypress tree.
2. Various kinds of valuable textiles imported from Cyprus.

D

Dabbit Couch or day-bed. (Yks)

Dabnet
1. Small fishing net for use in streams. (Oxf)
2. *Dobnet.

Dag Heavy hand-gun or pistol.

Dagswain Coarse coverlet of shaggy, rough material.

Damask A rich silk fabric, woven with elaborate designs, originally from Damascus. Later, a twilled table linen, with an elaborate design woven in, seen by the reflection of light; the term was subsequently applied to any fabric woven in this way.

Dannock Hedgers gloves: the left hand glove was left whole in order to grasp thorns; the right had fingers so that a bill hook could be used.

Dansk 16th century English for Denmark and Danzig; hence used of imports from the Baltic in general, especially goods made of spruce. Dansk chests sometimes incorporated marquetry work.

Dark Lantern *Lanthorn with a shutter to hide its light.

Dasher Detachable upright boards on the side of a wagon to increase its capacity, and to hold the load in place. (Ntt)

Dashin Tub for the preparation of oatmeal.

Dateler, Daytail Man One who works by the day; not regularly employed. (Northern)

Daubing Plasterwork; infilling of clay, dung or straw for timber-framed buildings.

Day Work Crops growing on an area of land that could be worked in one day, usually considered to be about three roods.

Dead Inanimate goods.

Dead-Eye Block with three holes through which a lanyard is reeved, to extend the shrouds on a sailing ship.

Deal A plank or board no more than seven inches wide and three inches thick.

Decretal Collection of papal decrees, forming part of canon law.

Defender Iron Iron fender in front of a fire.

Delf A large drain. (Lin)

Delft, Delph Ware Good quality blue and white tin glazed earthenware, of a type originally made in Delft.

Demath A day's mowing. (Chs)

Demicastor Felted hat, probably of beaver or other fur. (Lan)

Demiceint Girdle with ornamental work on the front.

Deposition A statement or testimony made under oath in answer to interrogatories, and recorded in writing, so that it can be read in court without the presence of the witness.

Derig *Dirige.

Desk Portable boxes fitted with locks for writing materials, letters, *etc.* Legs were added at a later date, to give the *standing desk, with a sloping, hinged lid, which could be used for writing.

Desperate Debts Debts which were unlikely to be recoverable, perhaps unsecured by *bond.

Deust Bed *Dust Bed.

Dey, Deyhouse Dairy. (Oxf; War)

Diachylon Ointment made from vegetable juices, applied with linen bandages.

Dial Surveyor's compass.

Diaper Twilled white linen cloth woven with geometric patterns, used as towels or napkins for drying hands during meals; also as table cloths. Originally made in Ypres, Belgium; hence the name (d'Ypres).

Diaper Ring Ring with a *diaper pattern.

Diascord, Diascordium A medicinal powder made from the dried leaves of *teucrium scordium* and other herbs.

Dicker The usual unit of exchange i.e. ten, in dealings in hides and skins.

Diet Daily food; may also refer to board, or to ones way of life in general.

Dight Dressed, prepared.

Dill A yellow flowering herb cultivated for its carminative seeds, i.e. as a cure for flatulence.

Dimidia One-half (Latin).

Dimity Stout cotton fabric with raised stripes or fancy figures, used undyed mainly for bed coverings and hangings.

Dinch Pick Three-pronged *dung fork. (Oxf)

Dintle A thin type of leather. (Lin; Yks)

Dirige Funeral service, from the Latin 'dirige', the first word in the Latin antiphon in matins, part of the office for the dead.

Dish The smallest dish of the pewter *garnish.

Dish Bink, Board, Cage, Cradle Rack or dresser for storing, displaying, and perhaps drying plates and dishes.

Dish Call *Call (1). (Yks)

Dish Ring Ring on which to stand hot dishes on the table.

Diss Type of grass from the Mediterranean, with fibrous stems used for making cords.

Distaff Cleft stick about three feet long on which wood or flax was wound for spinning by hand.

Dithe Cow dung cut and made into squares for fuel. (Lin; Yks)

Dobnet Cooking pot or small cooking utensil.

Docion, Doshan Vessel in which oat-meal is prepared.

Docking Iron Tool for docking horses tails.

Dod A stave or club. (War)

Dog
1. Fire-dog: bar supporting the end of a log, or on which a spit is turned in the fire-place.

2. *Andiron.
3. A type of clamp.
4. A lever for placing iron hoops on cart wheels.

Dog Iron *Dog (1 & 2).

Dog Wheel Treadmill operated by a dog to turn a spit.

Dole
1. Gift to the poor.
2. Strip of meadow land, the use of which is rotated annually.
3. Share, portion, or lot, e.g. of profits from a fishing trip.

Donge Mattress. (Nfk)

Door Doors were legally considered to be moveables and could therefore be listed in probate inventories.

Door Band *Band (4)

Door Piece Curtains covering a door.

Door Tree Door post or bar.

Dorman The fixed end of a joined table.

Dormant Table Table fixed to the floor in a permanent position.

Dornick A coarse variety of *damask: a silk, woollen or worsted fabric used for *carpets and *hangings, originally made in Dornick, Belgium (Tournay in Flemish).

Dorter Dormitory in a monastery.

Dossel Pannier carried by a horse.

Doubler A large bowl or dish, which could be of pewter, earthenware, or wood, sometimes used for making pies.

Doublet A close fitting garment, sometimes with detachable sleeves fastened at the armholes, and worn with *hose; the typical male dress, 16-18th c.

Dough Brake Machine for mixing and kneading dough.

Dough Cowl Cooler, generally wooden, used in baking.

Dough Kever, Trough Shallow circular tray or trough in which dough was mixed before baking.

Doules A nail sharpened at each end to fasten planks. (War)

Dovetail Joint Tenon joint shaped like a dove's tail, to fit a mortice of that shape.

Dow, Dowed Dull, faded, perhaps reddish-brown.

Dower The portion of a husband's estate allowed to his widow for life.

Dowl, Down Soft feathers used to fill the highest quality mattresses and pillows.

Dowlas A coarse linen or *calico used by the poor for sheets, skirts, smocks, *etc.* Originally from Daoules or Doulas, in Brittany.

Dozens Type of *kersey; coarse woollen cloth. (Dev)

Drab Un-dyed thick woollen cloth.

Draff Tub Tub for the refuse or grains of malt after brewing.

Draft Rake A large rake for corn or hay.

Drag
1. A heavy harrow for breaking up ground.
2. Sledge for transporting heavy objects.
3. Type of brake.
4. Butcher's hook.
5. Implement used in the hearth.

Drag Corn Oats and barley sown together.

Dragon, Dragoon A type of *carbine, so-called because it appeared to 'breathe fire' like a dragon.

Drall *Thrall.

Dram Dish Dish for serving small amounts of spirits or hot drinks.

Drape
1. Cloth, drapery; originally woollen cloth.
2. Sheep or cow being fattened for slaughter, especially one which has ceased to give milk.

Draught
1. A team of oxen or horses with their cart or plough.
2. Shaft of a *wain or cart.
3. A sledge. (Dor)
3. A measure of wool. (Oxf)

Draught Hook Used for pulling heavy weights.

Draught Net Fishing net.

Draught Yoke *Yoke (1).

Draw Bed An extending bed. (Lin)

Drawer Tool for drawing out nails.

Drawing Knife
1. Carpenter's tool for shaving and smoothing wood, consisting of a blade set at right angles to two handles, drawn towards the carpenter in use.
2. Knife for disembowling carcasses.

Draw Table, Drawing Table Extending table made with three leaves, the outer two sliding under the middle one when not in use; it may also have a drawer or cupboard underneath.

Drawn Work Fabrics ornamented by drawing out threads of the warp and woof to form patterns, perhaps also with needle-work.

Dray
1. *Sled.
2. Plough made without wheels or feet.
3. Cart without sides used by brewers.

Dray Blades Wooden slats beneath a *dray or sledge.

Dreap Barren. (Yks)

Dredge
1. A mixture of grains (usually oats and barley) sown together, sometimes malted for brewing.
2. An inferior barley.

Dredger, Dredging Box Box with a perforated top for sprinkling, e.g., salt, flour.

Dresser
1. A table or flat board for preparing food, dressing meat, or displaying plate or pewter; subsequently, a chest of drawers with shelves on top for displaying pewter.
2. Any implement or utensil used to dress or prepare objects, e.g. a shoemakers tool for preparing leather.

Dresser Board *Dresser (1)

Dressing Beam Work bench.

Dressing Board
1. Board on which cloth is laid to raise the nap.
2. *Dresser (1).

Dressing Box Box for toilet accessories, often with a small mirror.

Drift
1. Drove way for cattle.
2. Fishing net.
3. Ramming tool.

Drink Can A cylindrical vessell, not necessarily of metal, for holding drink.

Drink Stall A wooden stand for holding tubs, *etc.,* of drink.

Dripping Broach Spit.

Dripping Pan Pan placed under a *spit to catch drips from the meat.

Drug Saw Cross-cut saw.

Drugget A coarse woollen material, or perhaps mixed with linen or silk, felted or woven, sometimes printed on one side, and used for *wearing apparel, or for table or floor coverings.

Dry Barren, when it refers to animals.

Dry Hair *Hair Cloth.

Dry Vat, Vessel Container for corn, meal, and other dry goods.

Dubbing Board Board for dressing cloth.

Ducape Plainly woven, stout silk fabric, introduced by Huguenot refugees in 1685.

Ducat A gold coin in circulation throughout Europe, of varying value.

Dudgeon Dagger Dagger with a hilt made of dudgeon, a common box-wood.

Dudger Basket. (Gls)

Dulcimer A musical instrument; its strings are stretched over a trapezoidal sounding board, and struck by two hand-held hammers.

Dumb Waiter Serving trolley on wheels, resembling cake-stands, often of three tiers.

Dun Brown or greyish brown; a term often applied to horses.

Dung Fork, Hook Fork with crooked prongs for manure spreading.

Dung Cart Heavy two-wheeled cart for carrying manure to the fields, perhaps with detachable shafts, and able to tip.

Dung Crib
1. *Dung Cart.
2. *Dung Pot.

Dung Pot *Pannier with door at the bottom which could be strapped to a horse's back, used for carrying dung to the fields.

Durance A strong, durable cloth.

Duroy Common type of coarse woollen fabric. (Dev)

Dust Bed Mattress filled with chaff.

Dutch Chair A ladder back, rush-seated chair.

E

Eander *Andiron

Ear
1. The handle of a dish or pot.
2. The part of a bell by which it is hung.

Earth Made of earthenware.

Earwingle, Erwing *Windle Blade. (Sal)

Easement The right to use that which is not one's own, e.g. a right of way.

East Cloth Cloth from the Baltic, i.e. the Eastland.

Eatage Grass available only for grazing, especially the growth after hay has been cut.

Eatherhead *Netherhead

Ech, Eche Hook Hook on a cart or wagon which a rope passes through to hold its load in place.

Ecuelle A two-handled *porringer used for soup.

Eddish The second crop of grass, or the grass that grows on the stubble.

Edge Tool Sharp-edged metal cutting tools such as axes, scythes, bills, *etc.*

Eel Spear Two-pronged spear for catching eels by transfixing them as they lie in the mud.

Elbow Chair Chair with two arm rests.

Elden, Elding Fuel, brushwood, peat, *etc.,* for kindling fires. (Lin; Yks)

Elecampane The horse heal, a plant with bitter leaves and roots, and very large yellow flowers, used medicinally as a stimulant.

Elect One chosen by God for eternal salvation; the term used in wills usually signifies a Calvinistic belief in predestination.

Electuary A medicinal paste or conserve, mixed with honey, jam or syrup.

Ell, Eln A measure of length: generally 45 inches, although this did vary; often used to measure cloth.

Elledge A fluid measure. (Ham)

Elsin A shoe-makers awl, including its blade and haft or handle.

Elting Tub Tub for kneading dough.

End A measure of hops. (Wor)

End Iron *Andiron (2).

Engrain To dye a crimson or scarlet colour with cochineal.

Entail The right to property settled on several people in succession, so that none of them have absolute ownership - and hence the property cannot pass out of the family.

Entremet Side dish.

Entry Passage inside the front door.

Entry Fine Lump sum paid to the lord by a copyholder or leaseholder on entering his land at the beginning of a new tenancy.

Epergne Central ornament for a dining table, usually silver, perhaps holding pickles.

Erning Gallows Swinging *gallow tree. (Ntt)

Escript A written document; probably referring to deeds and muniments.

Escritoire Writing desk containing stationery and documents, often portable.

Escutcheon Shield or *hatchment, *etc.* on which a coat of arms is depicted.

Eshin Basin or *ewer for water or milk, perhaps made of ash wood. (Chs; Lan)

Estemenes Type of woollen cloth. (Dev)

Etch *Eddish.

Evell, Evill A three pronged fork; a type of dung fork. (Con, Dev)

Ewer Pitcher with a wide spout, particularly for water carrying, often used with a basin for washing.

Exe Axe.

Exhibition Grant to a university student.

Extinguisher A hollow conical cap for extinguishing candles.

Eye *Eythe.

Eye Wedge Small wedge for securing cart wheels when their iron rim was being put in place; or perhaps for securing the back of a cart.

Eythe Harrow.

F

Fages Remnant. (Wor)

Faggot Bundle of sticks bound together for the fire.

Falchion Broad sword, curved with the edge on the convex side; subsequently a sword of any kind.

Falling Band Band or collar worn flat around the neck, or a woman's veil.

Falling Board, Table Table which could be extended by putting up hinged flaps supported by moveable gate-legs; i.e. drop-leaf, or, alternatively, which was hinged to the wall, against which it lay flat when not in use.

Fallings *Hangings (2); *valance.

Fallow A pale-brownish or reddish yellow.

Fan A flat, fan-shaped wicker basket, or perhaps a specially designed wooden shovel, used in winnowing; subsequently, a mechanical device for generating a draught to separate the grain from the chaff.

Farandine Fabric of silk and wool or hair; a dress of this material.

Fardel
1. A small bundle or parcel.
2. The fourth part of anything, e.g. especially land.

Farm Amount due annually as rent or tax; may be applied to tithes, fines, *etc.,* as well as land.

Farthing
1. *Fardel (2).
2. A quarter of a penny.

Farthingale A framework of hoops, used to extend the skirts of a lady's dress so that they stood out from the waist. Fashionable in the 16th c.

Fash Tub Mixing tub. (Dur)

Fat *Vat or tub.

Faucet Stopper or screw-top for the vent hole in a cask; a beer tap.

Feal Heap Spoil tip. (Sal)

Feather Bed Mattress filled with feathers.

Feele Bedstead Bed with curtains hanging from a central point above to form a canopy. (Dev)

Fell Skin of an animal, including its hair or wool.

Felloe Curved wooden section of a spoked wheel.

Fellow A servant. (Sfk)

Felt Felt hat.

Fender Fire guard, preventing the cinders spreading from the hearth onto the floor.

Fennel A fragrant herb cultivated for its use in sauces.

Fenestral Small window, often fitted with paper, cloth or canvas rather than glass.

Fenugreek A leguminous plant, whose seeds are used by farriers, and whose leaves are eaten by both animals and men.

Feoffee Trustee invested with a freehold estate in land for charitable or other purposes.

Ferret Stout cotton or silk tape, used for garters, *etc.,* often decorated.

Fest To bind an apprentice. (Yks)

Festoon Curtains suspended between two points so that they curve gently.

Fetters *Horse Lock.

Fewster Maker of saddle trees. (Dby)

Feying Cloth *Winnowing Cloth. (Lin; Yks)

Feying Rake Rake for spreading manure or collecting rubbish. (Dby)

Field Bed
1. Bedstead with curtains hanging from a central point, forming a canopy, and covering the framework entirely with curtains and draperies.
2. Folding bedstead which could be folded up for travelling.

Filigree Decorated with thread and bead-work, usually of gold and silver.

Fill *Thill.

Fillet Head band or tape suitable for binding the hair.

Filleting Narrow ribbon or tape.

Filosella Worsted cloth of silk and wool.

Fimble The male hemp plant (formerly thought to be the female plant), which produces a weaker and shorter fibre than *carl hemp, and was used for making fine linen.

Finched Having a white streak along the back.

Finding Maintainance for a minor, a widow, or other dependent person.

Fine
1. *Entry fine.
2. Fee paid by a tenant to transfer or alienate his land, or for some other privilege.

Firdeal Plank of pine or fir, usually about 6 feet long, 9 inches wide and 3 inches thick.

Fire Box Tinder box.

Fire Curtain Fire guard or screen.

Fire Dog *Andiron.

Fire Elden *Elden.

Fire Fork A two-pronged tool with a long handle which could be used as a poker, or to put fuel on the fire.

Fire House Heated room, with perhaps the only hearth in the house, and therefore the main room.

Fire Irons Collective term for iron implements used in the hearth.

Fire Pan
1. *Chafer.
2. Iron pan placed under a grate to catch the ashes.

Fire Pike, Prong A long poker used in the hearth.

Fire Scummer Fire shovel for removing ashes.

Fire Skase Brass or copper hood with handle at the top, placed over a fire at night to allow it to burn without endangering the house.

Fire Slice Fire shovel.

Firkin Small cask for liquids, butter, fish, *etc.,* half a *kilderkin or a quarter of a *barrel.

Firth Timber Brush or hedge wood or wattles. (Dev)

Fish Garth Enclosure or weir for keeping fish in a river or pond.

Fish Kettle Shallow oval dish, with a lid, for boiling fish.

Fisken Rough basket. (Lan)

Fitchew Pole cat, or weasel, and hence its fur or skin.

Flacket
1. Small flask or barrel, holding about three pints, used to carry drink to or by field workers.
2. *Flasket.

Flag Rush, reed or coarse grass; rush or wicker-work.

Flageolet A small wind instrument with the mouthpiece at one end, six principal holes, and, sometimes, keys.

Flagon Large vessel with a narrow neck for holding wine or other liquors for use at table.

Flail Implement for threshing corn by hand.

Flake
1. *Flitch.
2. A wattle hurdle, sometimes used as a temporary gate.
3. A rack hung from the ceiling to suspend *flitches or bread, *etc.*

Flaming Red flannel, used for bedding and underclothes. (Dev)

Flanders Chest, Cupboard Oak chest or cupboard carved and ornamented in the Flanders style.

Flannell An open woollen stuff of loose texture, usually without nap.

Flask Case of leather, metal or horn for carrying gunpowder.

Flasket
1. *Flacket (1).
2. Shallow basket, with a handle at each end, used for carrying clothes.
3. A tub for washing clothes in, or for clothiers to size their warp.

Flat Broad, shallow basket or metal dish, for carrying produce to market, or for laying out food on the table.

Flat Candlestick Candlestick with a flat base and short stem, suitable for a bedroom.

Flat Iron Solid metal smoothing iron, heated beside the fire.

Flat Piece Shallow drinking cup.

Flaught Turf sod dried and used as fuel. (Yks)

Flaxam Similar to *buckram, but made from flax. (Chs)

Fleache, Fleake, Fleek *Flitch.

Fleam Farrier's lancet used for blood-letting.

Flesh Meat.

Flesh Axe Meat chopper.

Flesh Barrel, Bucket, Fat, Kit, Tub Container for salting meat for preservation.

Flesh Crook, Hook Hook from which *flitches were suspended, or which could be used to take meat out of a pot or cauldron.

Flesh Pick, Pike A long fork for handling hot meat.

Flew A small fishing net.

Flint Glass Lead crystal glass.

Flitch The side of an animal, usually bacon, sometimes beef, salted and cured, and frequently 'hung from the roof'.

Flitting Tye Stake for tethering animals.

Float
1. A broad shallow vat used for cooling in brewing.
2. Plasterer's tool for levelling the surface of plaster.

Flock Woollen refuse used for stuffing pillows, mattresses and cushions; also used to make a poor quality cloth.

Flock Bed Mattress filled with *flock.

Fly Leg Table Table with a flap supported by a moveable leg.

Fly Table Table with a flap supported by a fly rail or swinging bracket.

Focer *Forcer (1).

Fog The second crop of hay, or the grass which grows up after the first crop has been harvested.

Foins Clothing or trimmings made of the fur of the beech-marten, the polecat, the weasel, and similar animals.

Fold Bar *Fold Pike (Ntt).

Fold Course Area over which a flock of sheep could be grazed; a sheep walk.

Fold Flake *Flake (2).

Fold Pike Staff with an iron point, used to pierce the ground in making hurdles. (Lin; Yks)

Fold-up Bed Folding bed, probably used by servants or children.

Folding Table Table with a hinged leaf which rested on the other leaf when not in use.

Foldstead Fold.

Follower
1. That part of a cider or cheese press by which pressure is applied
2. Foals or calves dependant on their mothers, and hence 'followers'

Foot
1. An ale warmer; metal utensil that could be thrust into the fire.
2. A measure used in selling meat.

Foot Pace
1. *Carpet or mat. (Lin)
2. Platform or step; foot rest.

Forcer
1. A small chest, coffer, or casket, sometimes covered with leather, bound with iron bands, and with a lock, used for the storage of documents, jewellery, and other valuables.
2. The plunger of a water pump.

Forcet Small chest used for storing documents, jewellery, etc.

Fore Hammer, Forchamer Large blacksmith's hammer; sledge hammer.

Fore Plane Plane used to prepare wood for the smooth plane.

Fore Room The principal or front room of a house.

Forehead Cloth Band worn by ladies on the forehead.

Forest Bill A woodman's *bill.

Forest Work Cross stitch embroidery on *canvas, depicting trees.

Forkes Frame of a pack saddle.

Form
1. Bench without back support.
2. A stand for barrels. (Wor)

Former Gouge, used by carpenters and masons.

Forthbringing The carrying of a body to burial. (Northern)

Fossard, Fossett *Forcer (1).

Fother
1. Fodder.
2. Standard weight of lead or stone.
3. A load or large quantity of something, e.g. hay, wood. (Lin/Yks)

Fotheram The space behind the rack in a stable where hay is stored. (Dby)

Fountain Receptacle for water or oil.

Fowling Piece A long-barrelled gun for shooting game, with a narrow bore for greater accuracy.

Fowmared Polecat. (Yks)

Frail
1. A rush basket, used for carrying tools and meals to work.
2. *Flail.

Frame The legs and cross-rails of a table or bed; a supporting structure.

Frame Chair Chair on a frame, as opposed to a box.

Frame Lace, Lacework Lace made on a frame.

Frame Saw, Framing Saw Saw stretched in a frame to make it taut.

Framed Bed Bedstead with panelled foot, head, and possibly top; see also *Frame.

Framed Table A joined table, with the top fixed to its legs, stretchers, and top rails, rather than sitting on trestles.

Frampot Large pot used to collect vegetables from the field. (Chs)

Frandel A quarter of an acre. (Gls)

Frankincense An aromatic gum resin obtained from various different trees - fir, pine, etc., used for burning as incense.

Frate Hoop Iron hoops for a barrel or tub. (Bkm)

Frater Refectory in a monastery.

Freehold A tenure in which the tenant holds his land virtually absolutely in his own right, although there may be a notional lord.

Freestone Stone such as limestone or sandstone that can be cut or sawn freely without breaking.

Freith Wattle or brushwood for fencing. (Dev)

French Barley, French Wheat Buck wheat, grown for animal fodder.

French Bedstead Bed with a wooden framework; the corner posts were joined by rods on which the *hangings (2) were hung.

French Hood A hood worn at the back of the head, but curving forward over the ears. Fashionable in the mid-16th century.

French Teston A silver coin, struck in France by Francis I (1515-47).

Fret
1. Ornamental network of jewels and flowers.
2. Wicker basket.
3. Iron hoop around the hub of a wheel. (Dby)

Frieze Thick, coarse woollen cloth with nap on one side, used for outer garments.

Frill A small *ruff.

Fringe Ornamental border consisting of a narrow band with threads of silk, *etc.*, attached, either loose or formed into tassels or twists.

Frith
1. Land with sparse trees or underwood; a plain between woods; unused pasture land.
2. Young whitethorn, used for sets in hedges.

Fritter Pan Used for cooking fritters, or small pancakes with apples in them.

Frizado A fine kind of *frieze.

Frog
1. An oven fork or poker; a ratchet. (Lin; Yks)
2. Small *andiron.

Frommard Wood-workers' tool for splitting and quartering wood. Similar to a *cleaver (2), but smaller and with a handle.

Frontlet Ornament or band worn on the forehead.

Frost Silver grey colour.

Frundle A dry measure: two pecks. (Lin)

Frying Pan Designed with either long handles to enable the user to stay well clear of the fire, or with small rings so that it could be supported by pot *hangings (1).

Fuezee A light musket or firelock.

Fuller
1. One who finishes cloth.
2. A blacksmith's tool for grooving iron. (Oxf)

Fullers Earth Clay used for cleansing and de-greasing cloth.

Fume Pan *Perfuming Pan.

Furgon Poker. (Lin)

Furnace *Cauldron, originally hung over an open fire, but later set in masonry with its own fire; used for boiling or brewing.

Furniture Usually used as a general term to describe something set up for use, e.g. a horse's harness, a bed with all its coverings, a table with its *frame, and so on. Hence 'furnished', set up with all that goes with it. (South West)

Fur, Furse Furze or gorse, used as fuel.

Fustian A coarse fabric made from a mixture of cotton and linen, with a silky finish, used for furnishings and heavy clothes; conjecturally originating in Fostat, Egypt.

Fustic Two types of wood, both of which give a yellow dye.

Futs Phates: a measure of brine used at Droitwich.

G

Gaberdine
1. Cotton or silk material with a woollen lining.
2. A coarse loose frock or smock.

Gabert *Cobiron. (Oxf)

Gable Rope A large thick rope; a cable. (Dby)

Gad
1. Goad: a sharp pointed rod for driving oxen.
2. A bar of iron. (Dby)
3. A strip of open pasture, 6½ feet wide. (Lin)

Gaff Staff with an iron hook used by fishermen.

Gaffell, Gaffle Bow A steel lever used for bending a cross-bow.

Gage
1. Pledge or deposit to ensure that a particular action is performed, usually financial in nature.
2. Quart pot or bowl.
3. A measure of hay, or small load carried by a pack animal. (Dby)

Gait *Gate.

Gale A bull or boar castrated after reaching maturity. (Dor)

Gales *Gallows.

Gall
1. Ox gall, used in painting and pharmacy.
2. An excrescence from the leaves and young twigs of the oak, used to make ink and tannin, as well as in medicines and in dyeing.

Gallery Landing or passage.

Gallibank *Gallows.

Galligaskins Loose breeches or hose.

Gallipot Small, glazed, earthenware pots used by apothecaries for ointments and medicines.

Gallon Standard measure of capacity.

Galloon Narrow, close-woven ribbon or braid of gold, silver or silk thread, used to trim clothes or upholstery.

Gallow Baulk The iron cross bar in a chimney from which *crooks hung.

Gallow Crook, Hook *Crook used on a *gallow tree.

Gallow Tree Iron frame used to suspend pots above the hearth. Gallows were placed on either side of the hearth and could be made to swing into the required position.

Galloway Breed of small strong horses originating in Galloway.

Gallows
1. *Gallow Tree.
2. Braces used for supporting breeches.

Galosh Wooden clog, shoe or sandal, sometimes with leather uppers.

Gambadoes Boot-like attachments to a horse's saddle to protect the rider's legs and feet from wet and cold.

Gambrel Hook or forked stick used by butchers for hanging meat.

Gang A set, e.g. of wheels, *felloes, harrow teeth, *etc.*

Gantry Four-footed wooden stand for barrels.

Garble Refuse from spices.

Garde Room Lavatory or privy, with a wooden or stone seat, and a shute to ground level.

Gardeviance Small chest for holding valuables; also a safe for meat.

Garietes Leg armour; *greaves (2). (Ntt)

Garn
1. Provisions.
2. Yarn, i.e. spun fibre ready for knitting or weaving.

Garner Chest, storehouse, or small barn for grain or flour.

Garnish Set of table vessels - *saucers, dishes, plates and *chargers - made of *pewter; usually twelve of the first three items.

Garret Attic; room just under the roof, usually used for storage.

Garth Enclosed garden or yard, usually beside a house or other building.

Gassloch *Gaveloch.

Gate Right to graze an animal on the common pasture.

Gathering Tub Mash tun in which malt is added to brew beer; *mashing fat.

Gaubert The iron rack in a chimney supporting *pot crooks.

Gaud Ornamental trinket; originally one of the larger, more ornamental beads between a decade of aves in a pair of *beads.

Gauger Measuring instrument.

Gavelock Iron crowbar or lever; large fork; a spear.

Gawn
1. A gallon.
2. A ladle or pail holding half a gallon.

Gayle *Gallow Tree.

Gear Equipment, especially horse or ploughing tackle, but sometimes used as a collective noun for a variety of different things, including livestock.

Gears The small wires through which the warp is passed on the loom to separate the threads, so that the *shuttle containing the *weft could pass between alternate threads of the warp.

Geld Barren.

Gelding Castrated horse.

Gelt Sheep Castrated sheep.

Gemel, Gimmal Finger-ring that could be divided into two or perhaps three.

Gemew
1. Hinge.
2. Jaws of a bag opening on pins at both sides.

Genny Guinea fowl; turkey.

Gesse *Girse.

Ghostly Enemy The devil.

Ghostly Father Father confessor.

Gib Stand for a barrel. (Dev)

Gib Crook Hook for hanging meat.

Gibbet *Gallow Tree.

Gig
1. A winnowing fan.
2. A light, two wheeled, one-horse carriage.

Gig Mill Wheel Rotating barrel or drum, to which teazle heads were fixed. The barrel was rotated at high speed, whilst cloth was pulled under it in the opposite direction thus raising the nap on the cloth.

Gill Measure equal to one quarter, or, in the north, one half of a pint; vessel to hold this quantity.

Gill Pot, Vat Pot or vat to hold a *gill of liquid.

Gilt
1. Young female pig about to give birth to its first litter.
2. Overlaid with a thin coating of gold.

Gilt Leather Calfskin, faced with tin foil and glazed with a yellow varnish.

Gimlin Wide but shallow tub for salting bacon. (Ntt; Yks)

Gimmer
1. Young female sheep. (Dur; Yks)
2. *Gemew (1).

Gimp
1. *Camlet.
2. A type of mohair.
3. Coarse lace on a wire or twine foundation, used for trimming *wearing apparell.

Gimp Lace The coarser thread which forms the outline of the design in lace-making.

Gin
1. A machine or mechanical contrivance.
2. Horse operated device for hoisting or pumping in a pit.

Gingerline A reddish-violet colour, from the French 'zinzolin'.

Girandole An elaborate *sconce (1); chandeliers.

Girdle
1. A belt or chain worn around the waist in order to secure or to confine clothes, often with long ends hanging down, and sometimes used to carry a purse or a sword.
2. *Griddle.

Girdler Maker of girdles and belts.

Girse, Girth
1. Horse-girth: the leather band securing a saddle or pack on a horse's back.
2. Saddle cloth. (South West)

Girth Tub Hooped barrell.

Girts Coarsely ground oats. (Dev)

Gist The right to pasture cattle; *agistment. (Lin; Yks)

Githern, Gitter(n) *Cithern

Gladdin A type of flannel. (Chs)

Glaive A weapon; the term was applied at various times to lances, *bills, *halberts and swords.

Glass Looking Glass.

Glass Box, Case, Cupboard Storage furniture for glass-ware, hung on the wall and usually open, or perhaps with a glass front.

Glazing Wheel Wheel coated with abrasive material, used by cutlers for sharpening knives.

Glebe Land assigned to the support of parochial incumbents, as part of their benefice.

Glede Sandy-grey colour. (Yks)

Gloom Anvil. (Ess)

Go Cart Child's cart or frame on castors, used to teach toddlers to walk.

Gobbard, Gobert *Cobiron.

Goblet, Gobnet Drinking cup of wood, pewter, silver, etc., bowl-shaped and without handles; sometimes mounted on a foot and fitted with a cover.

Goddard, Godward *Goblet

Goaf, Goff A quantity of hay and corn stored in one bay of a barn. (Nfk)

Golbert *Gaubert

Gold Textiles made of gold thread.

Gold Weights Scales for weighing gold.

Goodman Courtesy term for men of substance beneath the rank of the gentry.

Goodwife, Goody Female equivalent of *Goodman; the mistress of a house.

Goose Pan Dripping pan; large stewing or cooking pan.

Gore A *butt (4) that is pointed at one end; a wedge-shaped piece of land on the side of an irregular open field.

Gorget
1. Throat armour; steel collar.
2. An article of female dress covering the throat.

Gorse Hook *Bill for cutting gorse or furze.

Gossip God-parent; a familar acquaintance.

Goule, Gowl
1. Payment to a superior. (Oxf)
2. A quantity of corn that can be made into a sheaf. (Oxf)

Gouty Chair Chair with a leg rest, for sufferers from gout.

Gown Garment with a large fur collar, which could be short or long. It was open at the front, often with pleats at front and back. Similar to an academic gown.

Gradual, Grail Book Book containing antiphons to be sung between the epistle and the gospel at the eucharist.

Grafting Saw Hand saw used for grafting.

Grain
1. Scarlet grain or cochineal; the dye from either of these, or dye in general; the texture of a garment.
2. Outer side of a piece of leather.
3. Seed from West Africa used as a spice and in medicine.
4. Refuse of malt after brewing, fed to swine or cattle.
5. Acorn.

Grain Staff Fork on a stick.

Grainer, Graining Knife Tool used by tanners and skinners for stripping hair from hides.

Grape Dung fork. (Dur)

Grapper Grappling hook; a nautical term.

Grat
1. *Bread Brake.
2. *Gridiron.

Grate Framework of iron bars holding the fuel in a fire-place.

Grave
1. Manorial officer. (Yks)
2. Spade for breaking up coarse land. (Yks)

Graver Engraving tool.

Great Chair Armchair with a carved, panelled back.

Greave
1. Brushwood.
2. Armour for the leg below the knee.

Greaves The offal of rendered tallow.

Gredel *Gridiron.

Green Ginger Undried root of ginger.

Green Sauce Sauce made from herbs, eaten with meat.

Gressum Entry fine paid on entering copyhold or leasehold property. (Yks)

Grey Pea The common pea.

Grice, Gris The fur of any grey animal.

Griddle *Gridiron.

Gridiron An iron grate or framework of bars, square or circular, with short legs and a long handle, for broiling food over an open fire.

Grinding Stone, Grindstone, Grindlestone Millstone, for grinding corn or perhaps minerals.

Grintern Place to store threshed corn; compartment in a granary. (Dor)

Gripyard A platting of stakes and twisted boughs filled with earth to confine a watercourse. (Chs)

Grise *Girse.

Grist Corn about to be ground, or when it has just been ground.

Grist Mill Mill for grinding corn.

Groaning Chair Chair for the nursing mother to sit on when receiving visitors after childbirth.

Groat Silver coins worth four pence issued between 1351 and 1662.

Groats, Grots Hulled and crushed grain, especially oats.

Grograin, Grogram Thick coarse fabric of mohair, wool, and sometimes silk; often stiffened with gum.

Gromwell Seed used medicinally.

Groove A mine-pit or shaft.

Ground Rack Rack for dung.

Growings Land let out for agricultural purposes. (Gls)

Growle Stand A barrel used for the fermentation of malt. (Lan)

Grubber A large harrow; tool for grubbing up the ground.

Guard Ornamental border or trimmings on clothing.

Guile *Gyle.

Guinea An English gold coin, first struck in 1663 for trading with Guinea, on the West African coast, from metal imported from thence; originally worth 20s, but from 1717, 21s.

Gum Arabic Gum obtained from acacia, used medicinally.

Gum Dragon Tragacanth: gum from the *astragulus,* used medicinally.

Gun Flagon Large ale flagons, frequently made of pewter.

Gurgeons Coarse meal; the coarse refuse from flour. (War)

Gyle
1. The quantity of liquor that is brewed at one brewing.
2. *Wort in the process of fermentation.

Gyle Fat, Tun, Vat Vat which holds the *wort whilst fermenting, after the yeast has been added.

Gyle House Brewhouse.

H

Haberdyne Dried salt cod.

Hack
1. Mattock, pick-axe, or large hoe.
2. Rack for drying cheeses or holding fodder.

Hackaber, Hack Hammer Blacksmith's hammer. (Oxf)

Hackbut *Harquebus.

Hacking Horse *Hackney.

Hackle Metal comb for splitting the fibres of hemp and flax, and making them straight and smooth.

Hackney Horse of medium size and quality used for ordinary riding; perhaps a lady's horse.

Hackney Saddle A riding saddle, as distinct from a pack-saddle.

Hair
1. Used in plastering walls and ceilings.
2. *Hair Cloth.

Hair Cloth A stiff, wiry cloth made of horse hair (taken from the mane and tail) and perhaps linen or cotton, which might have a variety of uses; e.g. the mat on which malt was spread to dry over a kiln, a sieve, the side of a *keep (1) (to allow ventilation), *etc.*

Hair Line Rope or line made of hair.

Hair Ranger Sieve made of horse hair.

Hake
1. Hook over the fire, from which pots hung.
2. *Heck.

Halberd, Halbert A weapon: a cross between a battle-axe and a spear, mounted on a handle between 5 and 7 feet long.

Hale Iron bar for hanging hooks. (Sfk)

Half Ewe A half-grown ewe.

Half Hake Small *harquebus or portable firearm.

Half Headed Bedstead Bed with short corner posts, head-board of medium height, and either no *tester, or a canopy covering only the head of the bed.

Half Pipe Measuring vessel, usually of the same capacity as a *hogshead.

Halfendeal A half-share; a moiety.

Halfling Half-grown, young animal. (Lin; Yks)

Hall, Hall House The hall of a house; its main, or perhaps its only room.

Hall Canvas Canvas used to make *halling or *hangings (2).

Halling Tapestry, or stained / *painted cloth used as wall *hangings (2).

Hallowmas All Saints Day.

Halme
1. A handle. (Oxf)
2. *Helm (2).

Hambargh The collar of a draught horse.

Hamborough A fine woollen cloth, originating in Hamburg.

Hames The two curved pieces of wood, which formed a horse's collar, with hooks to which the traces were attached, so that the horse's shoulder did the pulling.

Hammer Mandrel Implement with a hammer on one side and an axe on the other.

Hamper Large wicker basket with cover, used as a packing case for clothes.

Hanap Drinking goblet, especially one used by the chief guest.

Hanch Upright part of a gate to which hinges are attached. (Dev)

Hand Linear measure.

Hand Board Tray.

Hand Diaper Hand towel of *diaper.

Hand Hook A short iron book, with a wooden handle, used by tanners to move hides.

Hand Iron *Andiron.

Hand Mill *Quern.

Hand Screen Hand-held 'screen', intended to shield the face from the heat of the fire.

Hand Waiter Elaborate serving tray.

Hand Wiper Handkerchief (slang term).

Handkerchief Buttons Worn by lovers on their hats: a miniature handkerchief decorated with tassels and fancy buttons.

Handle Cratch, Handles, Pair of A *cratch in which teasles were fixed to raise the nap on woollen cloth.

Handle Stock Wooden handle.

Handler Pit for 'handling' or soaking hides in a weak solution of tannin.

Hanger
1. Loop or strap on a *girdle, for attaching a scabbard to carry a sword, or for carrying keys.
2. *Hangings.
3. *Hangles.
4. A short sword.

Hanging Cupboard A cupboard hung on the wall, rather than standing on its own, or perhaps a wardrobe for hanging clothes.

Hanging Glass Glass mirror hung on the wall.

Hanging Lock Padlock.

Hanging Press A wardrobe in which clothes could be hung.

Hangings
1. Iron hooks attached to the chimney breast, from which cooking utensils were hung over the hearth.
2. *Painted cloth or tapestry hung on a wall or bedstead.

Hangles Chains in a chimney from which pots and pans were hung on *pot crooks.

Hangrell For hanging bridles, halters, *etc.,* in a stable. (Ham)

Hanley Ware Earthenware from Hanley Castle, Worcestershire.

Hannaborough, Hanyburrow *Hambargh.

Happing Rough cloth, bed-clothes, wraps. (Dur; Yks)

Happintree Stumps in front of a wagon when the shafts have been pulled out; pole of a *coop (3). (Lin; Yks)

Hard
1. When applied to livestock, barren.
2. *Hard Corn.

Hard Corn Wheat or rye, as opposed to barley and oats.

Harden, Harne Very coarse linen cloth made from the *hurds of flax and hemp refuse; cheaper than ordinary linen, used for cheap sheets.

Harled Speckled or mottled, applied to cattle. (Yks)

Harness
1. The body armour of a soldier, whether cavalryman or foot-soldier; a suit of mail.
2. That part of a loom which shifts the warp threads alternately to form the shed.

Harness Press For pressing clothes.

Harnessed Mounted with silver or other metal.

Harnise, Hurns The device in a loom that raises and lowers the warp to form a shed. (Dev)

Harpsicord A keyboard instrument; the strings were plucked by quills rather than being struck by hammers.

Harquebus Short gun used by infantry; it had to be supported by a tripod or rest when being fired.

Harrateen A linen fabric used for bed curtains.

Harrow Heavy timber frame, set with *tends, and dragged over ploughed land to break up the clods or cover seeds once they had been sown.

Harrow Buns Cross-pieces of timber on a harrow, into which its *tends are set.

Hartshorn Products made from antlers: knife handles, *etc;* antlers could also be used to produce a liquid from which ammonia was obtained for smelling salts.

Hassock Clump of turf or matted vegetation, especially of coarse grass or sedge.

Hastener, Haster A stand or screen for concentrating the heat of a fire on a joint of meat during cooking.

Hatch, Latch, and Catch Lower half of a divided door, with its fastenings.

Hatchell Implement for hackling hemp, i.e. for combing and sorting hemp fibres; see also *Hackle.

Hatchet
1. A light axe with a short handle, for use with one hand.
2. A small row or cock of cut grass. (Oxf)
3. A mason's dressing hammer. (Oxf)

Hatchment *Escutcheon; a square or lozenge-shaped tablet exhibiting the heraldic arms of a deceased person.

Hauberk A coat of mail.

Haulm *Helm (2).

Haulmere *Aumbry.

Haver Oats. (Dur; Yks)

Hawding Stock pigs for breeding, not intended for sale. (Lin)

Hawkey A white-faced heifer or cow, or simply a cow. (Yks)

Hawser A large rope used for towing ships.

Hay Croke Central remnant of a haystack. (Dby; Ntt)

Hay Spade A heart-shaped spade, with a sharp edge, used to cut hay.

Head Cloth A covering for the head.

Head Piece Head armour, helmet.

Head Tow The loop on a plough to which the 'short-chain' or draft chain is attached. (Con; Dev)

Headstall, Headstand That part of a bridle which fits around the horse's head.

Head Stock The frame over a mine-shaft supporting the winding gear.

Healds Small cords through which the warp passes in a loom.

Healing Stone *Hilling Stone.

Heardes, Hewards Bundles of *tow (1) of a certain size. (Chs)

Hearying Barrel Barrel used in malting. (War)

Heater Metal box with wooden handles, heated by inserting hot metal strips, and used to keep smoothing irons warm.

Heck Rack, usually for hay and other animal fodder; may also be used for cheese.

Heckall, Heckle *Hackle.

Heder Male lamb of eight to nine months, before its first shearing.

Hedgebote The right to materials for maintainance of fencing.

Heifer A young cow, from one year old until she bears her second calf.

Heirloom Chattels left to the heir.

Helm
1. The haft of a hammer, spade or other tool; a handle.
2. Straw, especially when tied up in bundles ready for thatching.
3. A cattle-shed in the fields. (Northern)
4. A *belfry. (Lin)
5. A quantity of rye or oats.

Helm Balk Loft for storing *helm (2).

Hemp A plant of the cannabis family, from the fibres of which coarse fabrics and ropes were made.

Hemp Butt, Garth, Land Field for growing *hemp, usually small.

Hemp Line String made from spun hemp.

Hemp Maul Heavy hammer or *beetle, usually of wood, for beating the fibres of hemp.

Hemp Rack Frame for stretching hemp.

Hemp Stock Hemp drying frame.

Hempen Medium coarse home-spun linen made from hemp.

Hempot *Hamper. (Sal)

Hemptery *Hempen.

Hengels *Hangings (1).

Herbage The right of pasturage.

Herdes *Hurds.

Hereditament Property which descends to the heir under common law; any kind of property that can be inherited.

Heriot The render due to the lord on the death of a tenant, usually the best beast, but cash payments might also be accepted.

Hesp Hank of yarn, of a definite quantity.

Hewer Iron Reaping hook.

Hewing Blade Axe.

Hewke, Huke Cape or cloak with a hood, worn by women, and subsequently by men. (Lin)

Hey An enclosure.

Heyment Ring hedge. (Chs)

Hiere Picra, Pigre Purgative drug made from aloes and carella bark.

High Bedstead *Standing bedstead.

High Day Holy day; a festival day.

Hiller A covering, a lid. (Ntt)

Hilling
1. Covering, usually of beds, but occasionally of tables.
2. A roof.

Hilling Stone Stone or slates for roofing.

Hind A servant or agricultural labourer.

Hinge Lock Padlock.

Hip-shot Having a dislocated hip.

Hobby Pony or small horse.

Hock Monday The second Monday after Easter, when money was collected for the church and parish before the Reformation.

Hod Receptacle for carrying coal.

Hodge *Hog.

Hog
1. A pig, especially a castrated boar, raised for slaughter.
2. A yearling sheep, not yet shorn.

Hog Colt Young horse: a yearling foal.

Hog in Feeding Pig being fattened for killing shortly.

Hoggerel *Hog (2).

Hogshead Cask for beer and other liquids, usually holding 63 old wine gallons (equal to 52½ imperial gallons), as prescribed by statute in 1423. When used for liquids other than beer its capacity may vary.

Hogswash The swill when a hogshead is washed out; it was fed to pigs.

Holdfast
1. A small safe that could be locked. (Dur)
2. A vice, clamp, bolt or other device to hold something fast.

Holding Animals kept as stock for breeding, rather than for slaughter.

Holland Fine linen fabric (although it was sometimes coarse and unbleached); linen and cotton cloth glazed with oil and starch, originally imported from Holland where the soil was particularly suited to the growth of flax from which a high quality linen could be produced.

Holland Clome Glazed earthenware imported from the Low Countries.

Hollow Lace Braid lace used for edging.

Hollow Ware Bowl or tube-shaped utensils of earthenware, wood, or metal.

Holmes *Fustian made at Ulm, Germany.

Holster Cap Leather pistol case worn on the belt, or fixed to the pommel of a saddle.

Holt Plot where osiers or willows are grown.

Homper
1. Hammer. (Oxf)
2. Measure of six pecks. (Oxf)

Hone Whetstone for sharpening knives, *etc.*

Hook
1. Usually s-shaped for hanging pots.
2. Sickle.

Hooker, Howker Bote Fishing smack with one or two masts.

Hoop
1. A measure of corn of varying capacity.
2. A quart pot or tub bound with hoops. (War; Wor)
3. A finger ring.
4. *Hopper.

Hop Pitch Iron crow-bar with a thick square point, used to make holes for hop poles. (Ess)

Hopper, Hoppit
1. A basket, especially the basket in which the sower carries his seed; a *seedlip.
2. A cheese vat.

Horn Book *Battledore (1).

Horreum Barn or storehouse (Latin).

Horse
1. Frame or stand on which to place barrels, vats, *etc.*
2. *Trestles (1).
3. Wooden framework for drying clothes.

Horse Flesh
1. Reddish-brown coloured cloth.
2. Live horses (not dead ones!).

Horse Harrow *Harrow pulled by a horse.

Horse Hilling Covering for a horse.

Horse Lock Hobble or shackle for a horse's foot, to prevent it straying or whilst it was being shod; it might be of iron with the owners mark on it to establish identity.

Horse Mill, Milne Mill powered by a horse pulling a beam attached to gearing, and walking in a circle.

Horse Pistol Large pistol carried at the pommel of a saddle on horseback.

Horse Pot Round wooden vessel containing a quart or peck of grain.

Horse Tree Piece of wood to which the *swingletree of a harrow is attached.

Hose Breeches and stockings treated as a single garment, covering loins and legs, sometimes also covering the foot like a long stocking, and worn with a *doublet.

Hostry
1. An inn or lodging room.
2. An ostler's room.

Hotes Oats.

House
1. The whole house.
2. Room set aside for a specified purpose, e.g. the malt house, which may be inside the house, or an outbuilding.
3. The *hall.

House Coarsing Brick laying.

House Sward Land for a house.

Household Stuff Miscellenous items of household furniture and / or utensils.

Housewife Cloth Middling grade of cloth for various uses.

Housing Cloth Sheet placed on a horse's back under the saddle, or over the goods carried on its back.

Hovel
1. Storage shed or outhouse, usually without sides (although in Essex one was 'over the buttery'). Used to store farm implements and produce, or for cattle and other animals.
2. The frame or stand on which a rick of corn is built, or on which peas or hay can be dried, perhaps with a thatched cover.

Howre Leder Over leather, used for boat and shoe uppers. (Dby)

Hub
1. *Nave.
2. The hilt of a sword or dagger.
3. A small amount of hay. (Oxf)

Huckaback, Huggaback Strong linen fabric with a roughened surface, used for towelling.

Huckmuck A wicker strainer placed in the bottom of the *mashing fat to strain new beer.

Huckster Pedlar, hawker, or small shop-keeper.

Humber Grayling: a freshwater fish.

Hurden *Harden.

Hurds The coarser part of flax or hemp, separated with a *hatchel.

Hurl Hurdle. (Dev)

Hurst Staff Wooden staff.

Husbandman Smallholder; one who tills the land.

Hustlements Household goods and chattels of little value, not worth separate mention.

Hutch
1. Small, lightly built boarded chest, box, coffer, or cupboard, on legs (or perhaps hung on a wall), used for the storage of corn, meal, etc.
2. A trough.

Hyssop Aromatic herb used medicinally.

I

Ile Side aisle in a room, perhaps separated by a screen.

Ilte *Gilt.

Imagery Embroidered, painted or carved figures or decorations.

Implements A collective noun applied to things such as household furniture, stores, or utensils; may include animals.

Imprimis In the first place (Latin).

In Stuff Things belonging to the household, rather than to the farm.

Indenture Deed between two parties, written out twice on the same sheet of paper or parchment, and cut along an indented or wavy line, so that each party had a copy. Its authenticity could be judged by matching up both copies.

Inderkin Coarse German fabric made from poor hemp, used for towelling.

India Back Chair Chair with a high hooped back, carved with Indian ornamentation; the design probably originated in Holland.

Indigo A blue vegetable dye, originally from India.

Indument An ecclesiastical garment, robe or vesture.

Infield Land Land close to the farmstead, which is regularly cropped; arable land.

Ink Horn Ink pot, originally made of horn.

Inkle Coarse linen tape or braid, or the yarn from which it is made, much used for shoe-laces, girdles, garters, apron strings, *etc.*

Inning Harvesting; hence 'inned', harvested.

Inset Work Marquetry.

Intake A temporary enclosure, often taken illegally from the waste. (Northern)

Iorney *Journey.

Ioynt *Joint.

Ireware *Iron Stuff.

Iris Root Root of the Iris florentina, used powdered as a perfume and in medicine.

Irish Cloth A cloth of wool or linen.

Irish Stitch, Work White embroidery on a white background.

Iron
1. Iron rack for holding tobacco pipes in the fire to burn out impurities of tar, nicotine and carbon.
2. An iron weapon; a sword.

Iron Back Fire back, protecting the back of the hearth, and usually decorated.

Iron Bound Wheels Wheels with an iron rim to reduce wear.

Iron Chimney *Chimney.

Iron Goose Tailors smoothing iron.

Iron Lane *Lane.

Iron Stuff, Ware Various small implements and utensils made of iron.

Iron Team The chains used to harness oxen and horses to ploughs or wains, *etc.*

Iron Tow Chains or links for towing; see *tow (2).

Iron Traces Harness of long chains worn by the lead horse in a team; see also *traces.

Ironing Box Smoothing iron made of brass or steel with a wooden handle. It had a cavity to hold a heated piece of metal which formed the base of the iron.

Isinglass Form of gelatine obtained from fresh water fish, especially the sturgeon, used in food preparation for making jellies; also in the manufacture of glue, and for other purposes.

Italian Iron Cylindrical iron with a hollow for the heater, used for fluting or crimping lace, *etc.*

J

Jack
1. A mechanical device for turning a spit; either driven by weights, or actuated by the draught of hot air rising in the chimney (a *smoke-jack); anything else that has a mechanical motion.
2. A short, close-fitting leather *doublet, stuffed with *tow (1), and sometimes plated with iron fastened together with cords.
3. A large leather drinking vessel.
4. A handle.

Jack Back Strainer used to strain the *wort from the hops.

Jack Leg Clasp knife; a pocket knife.

Jack Towel Towel on a roller.

Jacobus Gold coins struck in the reign of James I, worth 20/- originally, but more later.

Jaconet Type of muslin, originally from India.

Jade A horse of inferior breed; one that is in poor condition or is worn-out.

Jag Measure of the amount of hay that could be carried by a pack horse or on a cart.

Jagger A carrier, carter, pedlar or hawker; one who carries goods by pack horse, and especially (in Derbyshire) lead ore.

Jake *Close barrell or stool; a privy.

Japanned Treated with a black resinous varnish or lacquer which hardens and dries when heated. An oriental style, but not necessarily imported.

Japan Glass Lacquered glass with Japanese ornamentation.

Javelin A pike or lance: a pointed weapon with a long shaft for thrusting.

Jean Twilled cotton cloth, originally a type of *fustian, from Genoa.

Jell *Deal, plank.

Jennet Carpenter's adze.

Jer Gear Pieces of iron.

Jerkin A short coat or jacket, often made of leather or frieze, worn by men.

Jersey
1. Fine knitted wool; worsted made from finest wool.
2. Worsted wool, combed and ready for spinning.

Jersey Wheel Spinning wheel for making *jersey, used for stockings, etc.

Jestern A light coat of mail, consisting of iron plates riveted to each other, or to some stout lining material.

Jet Large ladle used in brewing.

Jib *Gib

Joicing *Agistment

Joined, Joint, Joyned Beds, stools, and other furniture made by a joiner using mortice and tenon joints, fixed with pegs and dowels, rather than with nails; furniture with legs turned on a lathe.

Jointer A long plane used to dress the edges of boards for jointing.

Jointure Property granted to a wife for life, the grant taking effect on the death of her husband.

Joists *Agistment.

Journey One load; the amount of corn; etc. carried in one journey.

Joyces Joists: the cross pieces of timber comprising the framework to support a floor.

Julep Sweetened drink used medicinally.

Jump Coat A coat reaching to the thighs, open or buttoned at the front, with long sleeves, divided at the back to the waist. (Dby; Sts)

Justment Grounds *Agistment.

K

Kanstyke Candlestick.

Kart Ladder *Ladder.

Keams A hair sieve. (Bkm)

Kedger A small anchor or grapnel.

Kee *Kine.

Keech Cake of consolidated animal fat, to be made into candles by the *chandler (2).

Keele, Keeler A *cooler; a shallow tub for cooling milk or wort.

Keep
1. Storage cupboard for food, sometimes made of glass, usually with perforated bars or sides of *hair-cloth to allow air circulation.
2. The stop in a door frame.

Keeper
1. Sick nurse.
2. Device for keeping a clasp in place.
3. Fire dog or *andiron.

Keeve *Keive.

Keive Vat or barrel used in brewing, for washing clothes and bleaching, and for a variety of other purposes.

Keever
1. A shallow wooden tub into which cider was racked, or for cooling the *wort in the process of brewing.
2. Cover for a dish.

Keever Cart A tipping cart. (Chs)

Keeving Racking process in making cider. (Chs)

Kell Decking A wooden platform for standing a *keele.

Kelter Coarse cloth used for outer garments.

Kench
1. Strip of land in an arable field, containing a number of furrows.
2. A measure of wheat. (War)

Kendal Green woollen cloth from Kendal, Westmorland.

Kenten Fine linen cloth, originally made in Ghent.

Kerchief A woman's head cloth; a handkerchief.

Kersey Coarse narrow and ribbed woollen cloth, woven from long wool; shorter and narrower than *broad cloth. Originally from Kersey in Suffolk.

Kettle Open cooking pot with semi-circular handles on both sides to suspend it over the fire; sometimes covered and used for boiling water.

Kettle Pan Four-handled pan.

Kib
1. Tub for drawing water from a well. (Dby)
2. Thick, narrow spade for use in stony or hilly ground where a plough cannot be used.

Kid A bundle of faggots used for firewood, or perhaps to be embedded in a bank, beach, *etc.,* to give firmness to the ground.

Kidderminster Stuff *Carpets and wall hangings of *Linsey Woolsey material manufactured in Kidderminster, shewing a pattern formed by the intersection of two differently coloured threads.

Kilderkin Cask to hold 18 gallons of beer or 16 gallons of ale, in accordance with a statute of 1531/2; other commodities, e.g. butter, might also be stored in kilderkins of various sizes.

Kill
1. Kitchen.
2. *Kiln.

Kiln Oven or drying frame, usually for malt or hops. The malt was laid to dry on a *hair cloth, well above the fire which was of burning straw. Other types of fuel made too much smoke and tainted the malt. Also used for baking, burning lime, *etc.*

Kiln Hair *Hair cloth used for drying malt.

Kiln House Room or out-house for baking, or for drying grain, especially malt for brewing.

Kilp
1. Iron hook in the chimney from which pots are suspended.
2. Detachable pot handle.

Kilter *Furniture. (Ess)

Kimblin *Kimnel.

Kimnel Cask or tub made of upright staves hooped together, made by a cooper, and used for brewing, baking, salting bacon, *etc.*

Kinderkin *Kilderkin.

Kine Cows; *cattle, usually the milking cows in a herd.

Kine Vat Cattle trough.

Kings Iron Large wedge.

Kip
1. *Kipskins.
2. *Kipe.

Kipe Bushel basket, made of osier with twisted handles on either side at the top, broad at the base, narrowing towards the top, with a capacity of 70 lbs, usually for fish.

Kipskins Hides from large calves or small breeds of cattle, from which was derived a supple leather suitable for coat and shoe uppers, *etc.*

Kirn Churn. (Dur; Yks)

Kirtle
1. Woman's outer petticoat, short skirt, or gown.
2. A man's coat or tunic, reaching at least to the knees.

Kit Any hooped and staved wooden vessel with a handle or handles (perhaps fashioned from one of the staves), and sometimes a lid; used for holding or carrying milk, butter, fish, *etc.* or perhaps as a milking pail.

Kiver A shallow wooden vessel or tub.

Kiving Vat Large wooden tub used in brewing or in the dairy.

Knack Tub Tub in which bread is kneaded. (Dur)

Knead Cowl *Dough Cowl.

Knead Turnell A shallow oval tub or trough in which curds were kneaded to squeeze out the whey; or in which dough was kneaded.

Kneading Trough Wooden trough or tub on legs for kneading dough; it had splayed sides, and a partition down the middle, so that it could hold dough and flour.

Knechyn *Knitch.

Knee, Knie
1. Piece of naturally bent wood useful in wagon construction.
2. A large angle bracket.

Knell The church bells' slow chime when being rung for a funeral.

Knit Hose Hose that has been knitted.

Knitch, Knitchin A bundle of flax or hemp.

Knitting Table Table used in knitting.

Knop Ornamental knob, particularly on the end of a spoon.

Knot A quantity of yarn or thread.

Kye *Kine.

L

Lace Loop Lace with patterns of small net worked in.

Ladder
1. Framework added to the sides or back of a *wain to hold in large loads of hay, *etc.*
2. Frame in the form of a ladder for storing cheese.

Lading Piggin A *piggin adapted for baling out water from boats, *etc.*

Lags The dregs remaining in a cask, *etc.*, when the liquor has been drawn off.

Laid Trimmed, embroidered.

Lair Cowshed or shelter for livestock.

Lair Stone, Layerston Gravestone. (Northern)

Lamballe Fabric made in Lamballe, Brittany.

Lamb Tow Lambs' wool when shorn.

Lammer Amber.

Land *Selion or strip of arable in the open field; about half an acre.

Landirons *Andirons, or a type of grate if in the singular.

Lane Iron ring at the end of a plough to which the horse is yoked. (Lin; Yks)

Langsettle, Long Saddle A long wooden seat with high back and ends; a *settle (1). (Yks; Lin)

Lanneret Male lanner falcon.

Lanon *Andiron.

Lanthorn Lantern; from the Latin, *Lanterna.* A portable light, which might be carried on a stave, with metal walls and panels of horn, enclosing a candle.

Lapis Lazuli A silicate containing sulphur, giving a bright blue pigment.

Lapis Tutty Tutty: crude oxide of zinc, or calamine, used medicinally in a stringent ointment or lotion.

Lap
1. To cover.
2. To cut and polish cutlery.
3. Leaf of a table.
4. The end of a piece of cloth.

Lap Table Small board placed on the lap as a substitute for a table.

Larder Storage room for meat and other provisions.

Larking Bell Device to attract larks into a net. (Wor)

Larnder A wooden trough. (Dev)

Last
1. Wooden model of feet on which shoes and boots are shaped or repaired.
2. A commercial measure of weight, quantity or capacity.

Latch Pan Pan placed under meat being cooked to catch the dripping. (Sfk)

Lath Strip of wood used to form a wall or partition, and in building work; also used as a framework for slates and tiles.

Lathe A barn or cow-house. (Northern)

Lather, Lether Ladder.

Lathing Iron An iron cross used to hold cross *laths whilst they were being nailed to long *laths.

Latt *Lath.

Latten A yellow alloy of copper, zinc, lead and tin, similar to brass, but weaker; used for cooking pots, candlesticks, *etc.* Often hammered into thin sheets.

Lattice Structure made of *laths, used as a screen in windows without glass.

Latting Axe Axe for splitting wood for *laths.

Laund Iron
1. *Andiron.
2. Smoothing iron for laundering.

Lavatory Ritual washing of a priests hands at the offertory, and after cleaning the communion vessels.

Laver A metal wash basin or jug; a cistern, trough or conduit.

Lawn Fine linen, resembling *cambric.

Lay
1. Type of pewter.
2. A local tax or rate.
3. *Lea.

Lay Metal *Ley (2).

Layer Piece of wood used in laying a hedge.

Layer Net Net for catching game. (Dev)

Laystall Burial place.

Lazy Back A rod with serrated edges used to tip a *kettle without taking it off the *pot crook.

Lea
1. Measure of yarn.
2. Open land, usually grassland or pasture.

Lead
1. A large *cauldron, pot or kettle, not necessarily of lead (although it might be lined with lead), used in brewing or for various other purposes.
2. A *cistern (1).
3. A shallow lead tray used in separating milk.
4. Pigments, giving red and white colours.

Leading Strings Reins to help children learn to walk.

Leaf Very thin sheet of metal, especially silver or gold.

Leap
1. *Seedlip.
2. Half a bushel.

Leap Cloth Cloth for a basket, especially a *seedlip.

Learning Schooling.

Lease
1. Contract between a lord and a tenant, whereby the former grants land to the latter for a specified term in return for rent, usually an *entry fine, and perhaps a *heriot, *etc.* Also termed '*chattel lease', as they were *chattels which could be bequeathed by will, in contrast to freehold land, which could not.
2. *Leasow.

Leasow Pasture or meadow, which might be enclosed or common.

Leather Bottle Bottles made of leather, and coated with tar or pitch, for carrying beer or cider to the fields at harvest time.

Leather Jack Container for fluids; a *jack (3).

Leaven Yeast, added to dough to produce fermentation.

Leaven Tub Tub in which dough is fermented.

Leery Empty. (South West)

Lent Corn, Grain, Seed, Tilling Any spring crop, usually barley or oats.

Letch Vessel holding ashes for making *lye. (Dby)

Letching Knife Knife for cutting meat into strips known as 'letches'. (Wor)

Lettice Whitish-grey fur, resembling ermine.

Lettice Bonnet Bonnet made of *lettice, raised in a triangular shape over the head.

Leurey *Livery.

Lever Tourn Handle.

Ley
1. *Lea (1).
2. Alloy of tin and lead similar to *pewter. (Wor)
3. *Lay (2).

Ley Sword The beating up apparatus in a *loom. (Dev)

Lid Window shutter.

Life in Possession The 'life' named in a *lease currently occupying the property leased.

Lighter Flat-bottomed barge, used for unloading (lightening) ships that are unable to reach a wharf, and for transporting goods by water for short distances.

Lights for Hot Beds Glass cloches for the garden.

Lignum Vitae The hard brownish green wood of the Guiacum tree, native to the West Indies; the resin from it, used medicinally.

Limbeck Copper or glass apparatus used in distilling; a still.

Limber Shaft of a cart, *wain, or carriage.

Lime Weights The weights to tension the warp in a vertical loom at which the weaver stood. (Dev)

Linch Pins The pins which passed through the end of an *axletree to keep the wheels in place.

Line
1. The laced cord on the frame of a bedstead which supports the *bed, i.e. the mattress.
2. Flax or flaxen thread; the longer and finer fibres of flax or hemp. Hence 'linen'.

Line, Linen Wheel Small spinning wheel for flax.

Linen Cloth woven from flax.

Ling Species of salt-water fish, often dried or salted.

Linhay, Linney Lean-to barn, perhaps with two stories; the lower for animals and open to the weather, the upper for storage of hay, *etc.* (Dev)

Link(s)
1. Torch made of *tow and pitch, carried in the street at night.
2. Chains for hanging a pot over the fire.
3. *Fetters.

Linsey Wolsey Inferior, loosely woven, coarse cloth made from a mixture of wool and flax, originally from Lindsey, Suffolk.

Lint Flax ready for spinning.

Lintel
1. The horizontal piece of wood or stone at the top of a door frame.
2. Tares in corn. (Dby)

List The selvage, border or edge of a cloth, usually of different material from the cloth itself.

Litharge Protoxide of lead, used as a pigment.

Litster A dyer.

Litten A churchyard. (Ham)

Litting Tub A dyer's vat.

Livery A provision of food and drink, perhaps with lighting, taken to the *chamber at night.

Livery Cloak, Coat Cloak provided by a lord to his retainers, and marked by his emblem so that their allegiance might be recognised.

Livery Cupboard Small food storage cupboard, with a perforated door for ventilation, originally intended for the *livery, and kept in the *chamber. Sometimes it was hung on the wall; alternatively it might have legs. There might be a shelf with a canopy above the cupboard.

Livery Table Table on which *livery, i.e. rations, were placed, or on which a *livery cupboard stood; a side table.

Lives Term for which a lease lasted, i.e. until the deaths of the 'lives' named in the lease.

Load The specific quantity of particular commodities which customarily makes one load, e.g. 36 trusses of hay weighing 18 cwt; 40 bushels of wheat, *etc.*

Load Cart Carts with detachable bodies and two wheels, drawn by a single horse. (Ess)

Load Horse Pack horse. (Dby)

Lock A quantity of wool hanging together; the short wool or fragments from a fleece.

Lock Saw A long, tapering saw, used to make a place in the door for a lock.

Locker Small cupboard with a lock for keeping valuables; sometimes built into a wall, or within a larger cupboard.

Locker Board Table with a drawer or small cupboard beneath.

Lockeram, Lockram Coarse loosely woven linen, used for making shirts, *etc.,* by the poorer classes.

Lodging Bed Bed for an inn's guests, or for living in servants or lodgers.

64

Logger Log or block of wood fastened to a horse's feet to prevent it straying. (Oxf; War)

Logwood The heartwood of an American tree used to make a black or dark-brown dye; also used medicinally. So-called because it was imported in the form of logs.

Longbow The traditional English weapon - a six foot bow stave, with arrows three feet long that could be fired at the rate of six per minute.

Long Pepper Condiment made from the immature fruit spikes of various peppers.

Long Wheel Spinning wheel for wool. (Sal; Sts)

Longart Tail or end board of a cart or waggon.

Long Saddle *Langsettle

Loo Table Round table designed to play a card game called loo.

Loom
1. An open vessel such as a bucket, tub, vat, *etc.,* perhaps for use in brewing.
2. Machine for weaving yarn or thread into fabric by crossing threads known respectively as the warp and the weft.
3. An implement, tool, or utensil of any kind.

Loom Work Woven material; weaving.

Loop Lace Patterns of lace worked with a needle on a ground of fine net.

Lop Wood Small branches and twigs lopped from a tree.

Lorimer Maker of small iron ware, especially for use on a horse's bridle; a spurrier.

Lorry A flat wagon on four low wheels.

Losset A large flat wooden dish or tray, similar to a *voider (1).

Lount *Selion or strip of land, separated from other lounts by a ridge. (Chs)

Love Thin silk stuff much used for mourning clothes.

Low Bed *Truckle Bed.

Lowse Crook Implement for unyoking horses. (Dur)

Lozenge Board, Knife Used for making diamond-shaped tablets for medicinal purposes.

Luce A pike, i.e. the fish.

Lug Long stick, or pole; the branch of a tree.

Lumber, Lumberstuf Odds and ends; dis-used objects; superfluous furniture.

Lustre Glass chandelier.

Lutestring Glossy silk fabric, in which the lustre and crispness is produced by heating and stretching the warp.

Lye An alkaline solution used as an alternative to soap. Wood ash was placed in a tub with a perforated bottom, and soaked in water to wash out the soluble potash salts. Straw was steeped in the resultant solution; it was then slowly dried and burnt. The ash was rich in potash, and softened hard water on wash day.

Lymes The place where skins were steeped in lime and water to whiten them.

Lysten A coarse cloth or yarn. (Dev)

M

Mace
1. Spice made from the dried outer covering of nutmeg.
2. A knobbed mallet used to make leather supple.

Madder A herbaceous climbing plant with yellow flowers, which produces a red dye.

Made Ware
1. Garments ready made.
2. Ware made up of different materials.

Maid Applied to various inanimate objects, e.g. a clothes horse, a *trivet.

Maidenhair Various different species of fern, much used in medicine.

Mail, Mail Coat Armour made of chains or over-lapping plates.

Mail Pillion; Male Pillion
1. Saddle of *mail.
2. Leather or wooden saddle placed behind the rider for carrying a *male (1), i.e. luggage

Male
1. Travelling bag, wallet or pouch.
2. Heavy wooden hammer.

Maling Cords Ropes for a pack saddle.

Malison A curse or malediction.

Mall *Maul.

Malligo Raisins from Malaga.

Malt Mill Mill for grinding malt before brewing.

Malvesey Malmsey: strong sweet white wine from the Mediterranean.

Manackles Gauntlet.

Manchester Wares Cotton goods made in Manchester.

Manchet Fine wheaten bread.

Mandrel
1. Pickaxe, sometimes used in mining, with sharp points at each end.

2. Cylindrical rod around which metal is cast or shaped.

Manger The trough or box in a stable or cow shed, from which beasts eat.

Mangle A device for rolling and pressing cotton and linen clothing, *etc.,* after washing.

Mankeing Rake for clearing ashes in a bread oven. (Gls)

Manna Juice from the bark of the manna ash, used as a gentle laxative.

Mantel The piece of timber or stone above the front of the fire place, at the base of the flue; often having a shelf or mantelpiece.

Mantle
1. A loose, sleeveless cloak or overcoat.
2. Blanket of woollen cloth.
3. *Mantel.

Mantua Loose fitting gown worn by women.

Map, Mappe Tablecloth, napkins. (Dby; Dur)

Marble Worsted cloth interwoven to resemble marble.

Mariner's Slops Wide baggy breeches worn by sailors.

Mark Unit of account, i.e. 13s. 4d. - but not an actual coin.

Marking Iron Branding iron.

Marl, Marrell Type of calcareous clay used as fertiliser.

Marmelet Small *marmit.

Marmit Large cooking pot, usually iron, fitted with hooks for hanging over the hearth.

Marrow A companion, fellow-worker or partner. (Yks)

Marseilles Quilt Patterned cotton fabric resembling quilting.

Marter The fur of a marten.

Martinmas Beef Beef killed and salted at Martinmas (November 1) ready for the winter.

Mase *Mazer.

Mash Tub Horse Stand for a *mashing fat.

Mashee Papier mache. (Wor)

Mashing Mixing malt with warm water to make *wort, the first stage in brewing.

Mashing Fat, Keive, Stove, Tub, Vat The vat in which the process of *mashing takes place.

Mashing Rule, Stick For stirring the malt in the *mashing fat.

Maskalyn *Maslin.

Maslin
1. Mixed grain, especially rye mixed with wheat, used in bread-making; the bread made with this grain.
2. A metal alloy similar to brass; hence maslin ware.

Massard *Mazer.

Massicot Yellow protoxide of lead, used for pigmentation.

Mastic A gum or resin exuded from the bark of various trees, and used medicinally.

Mat Plaited rush or straw mat placed over the *cords of a bed; a mattress.

Match
1. Wick of a candle or lamp.
2. Three-yard long cord, soaked in pitch and tied around the waist of the musketeer, used to ignite gunpowder.

Matted Chair Chair with a rush seat.

Matted Chamber Room with matting on the floor.

Mattock A type of pick-axe used for loosening hard ground, grubbing up trees, *etc.,* one end of the blade was arched and flattened at right-angles to the handle, the other was spiked.

Mattress Generally a *tick stuffed with flock, chaff, straw or hair.

Mattress Cords *Cords.

Maul A heavy hammer or club, perhaps used as a weapon.

Maund
1. Woven rush or wicker basket with handles and two lids, used for carrying eggs and butter to market.
2. A measure of weight or capacity.

Maundy The ceremony of washing the feet of the poor, usually on Maundy Thursday in Easter week, by royalty or ecclesiastics, usually followed by the distribution of food, clothing or money.

May Butter Unsalted butter, made in May to salve wounds.

Mazarine A flat pierced plate, fitting into a larger dish, for straining water from boiled fish, *etc.;* a deep pie plate.

Mazer A hard wood, used for making formal drinking cups or ornamental bowls; the cups themselves, which might also be made of maple or other hard wood, usually mounted on silver or gold; at a later date they might be made entirely of precious metals.

Meal Ground grain; tub for storing it, or measure of it.

Meal House, Loft *Boulting House.

Mean Field A field held in common, or in equal shares. (Chs;Lan)

Meat Food, diet - not necessarily meat.

Meat Board Dining table.

Medley, Medley Cloth Cloth woven from wool of various colours.

Melch *Melch.

Mell *Maul.

Mercer Dealer in textiles, *etc.*

Mercery Collective term for the goods sold by a *mercer: fabrics of all kinds, as well as groceries.

Merchantry Ware Trade stock; merchandise.

Mercury Precipitat & Sublimat Quicksilver, use medicinally.

Mere
1. A boundary.
2. A measure of land containing lead ore. (Yks)

Mess of Pewter Set of pewter dishes.

Messuage Legal term for a dwelling house, with its outbuildings and land; originally, that portion of land intended to be or actually occupied by a dwelling house and its appurtenances.

Met A measure of capacity. (Dby; Ntt)

Midden Dung heap.

Milch Milk.

Milch Kine Milking *kine.

Milk Boy Milk pail. (Dby)

Milk House Dairy.

Milk Spence Milk can. (Yks)

Milk Trunk Vessel into which milk was poured to be carried home from the field.

Mill In probate inventories, usually a hand-mill or *quern for grinding malt or mustard.

Mill Pick Tool used for cutting grooves in, or corrugating, millstones.

Mill Puff Type of *flock, used for stuffing mattresses. (Gls)

Millaine Coarse fabric made in Milan.

Millwell Cod fish.

Mind Requiem mass in commemoration of a deceased person, on the anniversary of the funeral.

Mingled Stuff Fabric woven from differently coloured threads.

Minikin
1. A plain weave worsted cloth, similar to baize.
2. A type of cotton.

Miniver A type of fur used as lining and trimming.

Mithridate A composition of various ingredients used as an antidote to poisons and infectious diseases.

Mitt Tub or half barrel used for kneading dough, or for handling curds in cheese-making. (Sal)

Mittons Gloves worn by a hedger to protect the hands from briars, *etc.*

Mixen Place for storing manure; a dunghill.

Mizzen Sail set on the mizzen mast.

Moarth Lard or fat. (Con; Dev)

Mob Close-fitting cap with two lappets; a woman's night-cap.

Mockado A fine cloth, originally made of mohair, but subsequently of either silk and wool, or silk and linen, with a pile surface. It originated in Flanders, and was made by Huguenot refugees in Norwich. Much used for clothing.

Mohair Fine type of *camlet, closely woven, originally from the hair of angora goats, but later from silk or other fibres. It has a lustrous wavy pattern or finish.

Moiety A half; one of two or more parts; a portion.

Molette Pair of pincers. (War)

Mona Dram Chest and stand.

Mongcorn *Maslin (1). (Gls)

Monks Chair Table chair.

Monteith Punch bowl with notches around its edge for suspending drinking glasses in water.

Months Mind *Mind, held one month after death. Legacies to pay for the candles used in this service are often included in pre-reformation wills.

Moorstone Granite used in the construction of *troughs, *etc.,* as well as for house building. (Con)

Morde *Moarth

Moreen Woollen, or woollen and cotton, fabric, imitative of mohair.

Morella, Morlay A material used for dresses, curtains, *etc.*

Moringe Axe Two-edged axe for rooting out stumps; a pick-axe. (Gls)

Morion Steel helmet, without a visor or beaver.

Morocco Goat leather, tanned with sumach, used in bookbinding and for fine upholstery.

Morris Pike Type of pike, supposedly of Moorish origin.

Mortar Vessel used to hold ingredients whilst being pounded with a *pestle.

Morte *Moarth.

Mortmain Lands granted in perpetuity to an ecclesiastical body or other corporation.

Mortuary Customary 'gift' paid to the incumbent on the death of a parishioner, or to an ecclesiastical dignitary on the death of a priest within his jurisdiction.

Moss Room Rights on a 'moss', i.e. an area of moorland, e.g. to take turves, sand, gravel *etc.*, to pasture beasts. (Chs)

Mother Corn Payment to the miller, by way of a proportion of the corn he has ground. (Dby)

Motley Cloth of mixed colours. (Lan)

Mould Loose or broken earth; surface soil.

Mould Rake Rake in the plough.

Mould Screen Cloche or garden frame.

Mould(ing) Board
1. A board or table for kneading dough in bread-making.
2. The board or metal plate on a plough which turns over the furrow slice.

Moulds Mens padded drawers. (Ham)

Mourning Cap Cap worn by a widow in mourning.

Mourning Gloves Gloves to wear in mourning.

Mouse Snatch Mousetrap.

Mourning Ring A ring to be worn by a widow during the period of mourning for her husband.

Mow A stack or rick of hay, corn, *etc.*

Mow Barton, Mowhay Stack yard.

Mow Stack *Rick Staddle.

Muck Crate Wooden pannier for carrying manure to the fields on horse-back.

Muck Drag, Hook Fork or implement with hooked tines for moving manure.

Mug Drinking vessel with a handle but no lid.

Mullen Bridle or head-gear for a cart-horse, with blinkers. (Oxf)

Mullet
1. Tweezers or pincers.
2. Grindstone or millstone for use by an apothecary or painter.

Mullock Rubbish.

Multer *Mother Corn.

Muncorn *Maslin (1).

Mung Mixed food for horses: barley, oatmeal, bran, *etc.* (Northern)

Munger Horse collar made of twisted straw.

Muntin The central vertical piece of wood between two panels.

Murdering Piece A wide bored hand gun which could be loaded with small pieces of metal to create a shrapnel effect when fired.

Murrey Mulberry coloured, i.e. purple-red; cloth of this colour.

Murrian *Morion.

Musketoon A short musket with a large bore, used by infantry.

Muslin Delicately woven cotton fabric.

Mustard Ball, Mill, Quern Hand-mill or *quern for grinding mustard seed.

Musterdevillers A mixed grey woollen cloth, originally produced in Montivilliers, Normandy.

Mydosalt, Mydsalt A salt meadow or salt marsh, where sea-water is collected for the extraction of salt. (Lin)

Myrabalan An astringent plum-like fruit, used for medical purposes.

N

Nag Small riding-horse or pony.

Nager *Auger. (Lan)

Nail Bore, Passer, Percer Gimlet or bradawl.

Nail A measure of length for cloth, about 2¼".

Nankeen Crude blue and white, or richly enamelled, porcelain from Nanking in China.

Napery Household, and, especially, table linen.

Napkin
1. A table napkin, essential when food was eaten with the fingers.
2. A pocket handkerchief.

Napron Apron.

Nathe *Nave.

Nave Wheel hub, into which the *axle tree is inserted, and from which the spokes radiate.

Neat A cow, calf, ox, bullock, *etc.;* cattle.

Neckerchief, Neckinger, Neck Rail *Kerchief worn around the neck.

Neeld, Nelde Work Needle work.

Nest of Boxes Chest of small drawers, as used by an apothecary.

Nether House Low service room or outhouse.

Netherhead Board at the rear of the cart which had to be let down when loading, or which could be extended to take an extra load. (Chs; Lan)

Netherstocks Silk or woollen stockings worn below breeches or hose.

Nets and Engines Devices for trapping birds, animals, vermin, *etc.*

New Sixpence Coins with a milled edge, following the re-coinage of 1696, contrasted with *old money.

Nib
1. Grip on a scythe handle.
2. The shaft of a wagon.

Nigella Romana Seed of Ranunculus, used medicinally.

Niggard False bottom for a grate, reducing fuel consumption.

Night Cap Skull cap with close upturned brim worn in bed.

Night Stool *Close barrell for use at night.

Night Table Bed-side table.

Nimes Thread Type of thread originally made in Nimes.

Nine An indefinite period between a week and a fortnight. (Sal)

Nipper Pincers, forceps or pliers.

Noble *Angel.

Noddie A light two-wheeled hackney carriage.

Nog
1. Small block of wood.
2. Handle of a scythe.

Noggen Coarse fibres of flax or hemp; or rough linen made from it.

Noggin Drinking cup, usually holding a quarter pint and made of earthenware; also refers to the quantity it holds.

Noil Short pieces and knots of fibre combed out of wool; wool refuse.

Nonage Under age, being a minor.

Normandy Canvas, Cloth Canvas cloth from Normandy.

Notary A person publicly authorised to draw up and witness legal documents, *etc.,* a commissioner for oaths (commonly abbreviated 'N.P.', i.e. notary public).

Notary Hole Pigeon hole. (Gls)

Nowt Cattle, oxen. (Yks)

Nuncupative Used of wills which were declared verbally, but not written until it was too late for the deceased to sign them.

Nun's Thread A fine cotton thread, for sewing.

Nut Cup made from, or resembling, a coconut shell, mounted on a metal foot.

Nut Coffer *Coffer made of walnut.

Nycette A breast cloth or light wrapper for the bosom and neck.

Nyld Needle.

O

Oad *Woad

Oakum
1. The coarse flax separated in hackling: *hurds or *tow (1).
2. Light fibres obtained by picking old rope, and used to caulk ships' seams

Obit A commemorative mass held on the anniversary of a persons death.

Oblation Gift to the church.

Obligation A legal agreement whereby a person becomes bound to another for the payment of a sum of money or performance of some service.

Occamy An alloy resembling silver, perhaps made of copper, tin and zinc. The word is a corruption of 'alchemy'.

Occupation Use.

Offal Iron Iron odds and ends.

Offal Wood Waste wood: the trimmings of trees that have been felled; small pieces of wood for kindling.

Ogee A doubly curved moulding, convex above, concave beneath.

Oil Cloth Waterproofed table cloth.

Oil de Bay Oil from the bay laurel.

Oil of Spike Oil from *lavendula spica,* used in painting, and for veterinary purposes.

Old Money Coins minted before the 1696 re-coinage. After that date coins had milled edges to prevent them being clipped by forgers. Old money remained legal tender until 1733.

Oleron A coarse fabric perhaps originating in Oleron, France.

Olive Wood Wood of the olive, used in ornamental woodwork as it could be highly polished.

Ombres Large cupboard in a stable for horse tackle. (Chs)

Orcanet A dye, obtained from alkanet.

Orchel A red or violet dye obtained from certain lichen.

Ordinary A variety of *kersey.

Orfray, Orphrey Rich embroidery, often gold, especially on ecclesiastical vestments.

Oriel Large windowed recess, often projecting from an upper storey.

Ormolu Gold or gold leaf prepared for gilding.

Orpharion A large instrument with six to nine strings, played with a plectrum, and similar to a lute.

Orris Lace patterned with gold or silver; embroidery made with gold lace.

Orris Root *Iris Root

Osmund Iron of a superior quality, used for arrow-heads, fish-hooks, *etc.,* originally imported from the Baltic.

Osnaburg Coarse linen originally made in Osnabruck.

Ostrey Hostelry: inn.

Otter Stave Long pole used in hunting otters.

Ottoman Cushioned seat for reclining, without back or sides.

Ouch Ornamental buckle or brooch, used to hold clothing together, and/or worn as an ornament.

Out Shot Out-building or lean-to (Northern).

Outing Vat *Uting Vat.

Outnal Brown flaxen thread from Oudenarde.

Over Leather For making shoe uppers.

Overbody Garment worn over bodice.

Overland
1. Land without a dwelling house. (Dev)
2. Land on the margins of commons or demesne land, that did not belong to a particular tenement, and that had no common rights attached to it. (Dev)

Overlay
1. Coverlet or cloak, cravat or neckcloth.
2. Harness for a pack horse. (Chs)

Overseer Person appointed to supervise the carrying out of the terms of a will. Overseers of the poor are rarely mentioned in probate records.

Overthwart Saw Cross-cut saw.

Ower Slag Refuse of lead ore. (Dby)

Owl A covered cup in the shape of an owl.

Owler Wood Alder wood. (Northern)

Ox, Oxen Any bovine animal, but particularly a castrated bull used as a plough-beast or for haulage purposes.

Ox Bow U-shaped rod usually made of ash, which passed under the ox's throat and up through two holes in the yoke above, to hold the yoke in place.

Ox Drag *Drag drawn by oxen.

Ox Rack Manger for oxen.

Ox Stall Stable for oxen.

Oxgang Measure of land, c.10-20 acres varying by locality; an eighth of a carucate or ploughland.

Oyster Table Table with a water-resistant top such as slate or metal used in the parlour for the preparation and eating of oysters.

P

Pack A bundle of anything bound up together; a container for carrying goods on horse-back.

Pack Cloth A cloth to wrap goods up for carriage, or to place under the *pack saddle.

Pack Saddle Saddle with straps for carrying loads on the back of a pack horse.

Pack Saddle Tree Rack for pack saddles.

Pack Thread Twine or thread used for tying up packs or bundles.

Pad
1. A bundle of straw to sleep on.
2. *Panel (1).
3. A soft saddle or small cushion for a *pillion.

Padaway A type of say or serge made in Padua.

Paddle Small spade-like implement for cleaning a *plough share of earth and clods.

Paddle Staff, Stave
1. A long staff with an iron spike or small spade at its end, used by mole catchers, and also as a walking stick.
2. A spade-shaped implement used to mash the *wort in brewing.

Painted Border A painted plaster frieze between the *wainscot and ceiling.

Painted Calico *Calico with painted designs or pictures, in various colours.

Painted Cloth Decorative wall hangings (to keep out draughts) or bed coverings, depicting religious scenes, mottoes, flower patterns, *etc.,* painted in oils, and usually made of cloth or canvas. A cheap substitute for tapestry.

Painters Black Black paint, dye, pigment or varnish.

Painters Oil Linseed oil.

Painters Stone Grinding stone for grinding up substances to make pigments.

Pair of Ruffs *Ruffs worn on the wrist.

Pair of Stairs A flight of steps, or a staircase with two landings.

Pair of Tables The two folding leaves of a table on which games such as backgammon are played.

Paise A weight, or a container to hold that weight.

Pale Stake or strip of wood for fencing; often 'pales and rails'.

Pall Cloth Cloth to cover an altar or a coffin.

Pallet, Pallias Straw-stuffed mattress; a mean or poor bed or couch.

Pampilion A coarse woollen fabric with a rough surface.

Panade A large knife.

Pancheon
1. A large, shallow, earthenware bowl, in which milk was allowed to stand in order to allow the cream to separate.
2. Cask with a quarter barrel capacity.

Paned Strips of differently coloured cloth joined together.

Panel, Pannal
1. A piece of cloth placed under a saddle, or lining the saddle, to protect the horse's back from chaffing.
2. A wooden saddle for an ass; a crude form of saddle.
3. A pack saddle.
4. That part of *wainscot consisting of a thinner board set into the main framework.

Pannier A large light basket for carrying produce to market on a horse's back; a saddle bag.

Pantofle Footwear of various kinds, e.g., slippers, out-door overshoes.

Pap Pan Pan used to keep food and drink warm.

Pap Spoon Spoon for feeding infants semi-liquid or mashed food.

Paper Chamber Room with *paper hangings.

Paper Hanging Wall hanging, usually printed with ornamental designs; wallpaper.

Paper Window Window with oiled paper in the place of glass.

Paragon Rich double *camlet, used in upholstery; originally from the East.

Parcel Piece or quantity of things, e.g. a piece of land of indefinite quantity.

Parcel Gilt Lightly or partly gilded silver, often having inner surface gilded.

Parell *Apparell.

Parchment Lace A type of lace, the core of which was parchment.

Paring Iron, Knyfe Used for shaving skins in tanning, paring off edges, or for paring a horse's hooves.

Pariswork A fine linen used for *napery.

Paritor *Apparitor.

Parlour Private sitting room used as a best room on special occasions, or as a best bedroom.

Parmacety *Spermaceti.

Partizan A pike with a long, double-edged blade, with various projections on each edge, which were mirror images of each other.

Partlet Woman's neckerchief, collar or *ruff, perhaps to fit the low neckline of a dress, and perhaps of transparent gauze. Originally worn by both sexes.

Pash Poker. (Northern)

Pashell Pestle, *beetle, or mallet.

Passement Gold or silver lace trimming.

Passer A drill or gimlet, *etc.,* for boring small holes.

Paste, Paste Board Sheets of paper pasted together as a substitute for a board.

Patch Box A box containing the small black patches which it was fashionable to apply to the face.

Paten Shallow dish on which the bread used at the eucharist is placed.

Paternoster A rosary, and especially that bead on a rosary which indicates that the Lord's prayer is to be said (from the Latin for 'Our Father').

Pate Skin from a calf's head.

Patté A cross on which the arms are almost triangular, meeting at the centre, and forming almost a square; similar to the Maltese Cross.

Patten Flat wooden clog, raised off the ground by an iron ring which kept the wearer from sinking into the mud.

Patty Pan Tin for baking small pies, tarts or pasties.

Pavement Could be used to refer to stone flags used as flooring inside a house, as well as to an outdoor path.

Pax Tablet or board bearing a symbol of Christ, the Virgin Mary, or one of the saints, kissed by the priest and congregation before communion.

Pay of the Parish Poor relief.

Pea Haulm Used for thatching and litter.

Peas Hook Hook for lifting pea haulms.

Peal, Peel
1. Paddle-shaped blade with a long handle, used for placing and removing bread, cakes, pasties *etc.* into and from the oven.
2. Pillow.

Pearling Type of lace for trimming the edges of garments.

Pearling Cat A utensil like a funnel used to coat *comfits with sugar.

Peason Plural of pea.

Peat Piece of turf cut for fuel.

Peck
1. Measure of capacity for dry goods: two gallons or a quarter of a bushel; a vessel able to hold that amount.
2. Raw skin of a sheep. (Sal)

Ped A wicker pannier; a hamper with a lid, perhaps to carry mackerell. (Nfk)

Peeling Thin fabric or skin used as dress material.

Pell *Pale.

Peltry Rack or place where undressed hides were stored.

Pelt Undressed skin of a sheep or smaller animal.

Pembroke Table Small table on four legs with hinged flaps which could be raised to make it larger.

Penal Bill Written *obligation to pay a fixed amount of money by a certain date, with legal penalty for non-compliance.

Pengjerd *Porrenger.

Penide A stick of barley sugar, used as a remedy for colds.

Penistone Coarse woollen cloth for garments, made in Penistone, Yorkshire.

Pennant Sandstone from South Gloucestershire used as building material.

Penny Small coin, worth one-twelfth of a shilling; made of silver until the reign of Charles II.

Pentis, Penthouse A shed on the side of a house, especially one belonging to a smithy, where horses stood to be shod.

Pepper Corn, Powne, Quern Hand-mill for grinding pepper.

Percer
1. Rapier or short sword. (Dur)
2. Any implement for piercing holes, e.g. an *auger, a gimlet.

Performed Fully set up, complete; e.g. a bed performed, a musket performed. (Con; Dev)

Perfuming Pan Pan in which to burn incense, to fumigate, scent, or disinfect.

Perk Wooden frame over which cloth was drawn so that it could be thoroughly examined.

Perpetuana Durable, glossy, wool fabric.

Perry Drink made from pears.

Persian Thin light silk for linings.

Perters Appurtenances. (Gls)

Peruke A wig, usually long.

Pestle and Mortar A pounding implement and bowl.

Petronel A large pistol or carbine often used by cavalry; the butt rested on the chest when firing.

Petticoat
1. A woman's skirt worn externally.
2. A man's small coat, worn beneath the *doublet; a waistcoat.

Pewter A grey alloy of tin, lead, and sometimes other metals, used for dishes and plates, *etc.*

Pewter Frame Shelves for displaying pewter.

Pewter Ring Stand Metal circle on which a hot dish could be stood.

Phatt
1. Lead receptacle used for evaporating brine at Droitwich. (Wor)
2. *Vat.

Philemort Feuillemorte: a tawny colour.

Philip & Cheyney Gloss woollen and silk cloth; kind of worsted stuff of common quality.

Philltugs Two pieces of wood on a horse's collar, fastened by leather straps; chains were attached to each piece for the horse to pull its load.

Piano Nobile The main storey, containing the principal reception rooms, of a gentleman's house.

Pick Pointed, pronged or forked implement for fireside or agricultural use.

Pickell, Pike Evil Pitchfork

Picking Hammer Tiler's hammer. (Nfk)

Pie Rules governing the occurrence of more than one 'office' falling on the same day, for the use of clergy.

Pie Crook Pie plate.

Piece The weight or balance of a clock.

Pied Parti-coloured: of two or more colours.

Pier Glass Tall, narrow mirror, placed on the 'pier' between two adjoining windows.

Pig Iron A flat plate of iron hung on bars between the spit and the fire, when the latter is too hot.

Piggin Small wooden milk-pail, with one stave longer than the rest to serve as a handle.

Pightle Small field or enclosure; a close or croft.

Pig's Darn A sow.

Pike
1. Pick or pitch-fork.
2. A very long staff with a spear on its head, carried by infantry (pikemen).
3. Temporary hay-stack in the fields, peaked to let the rain run off. (Dur)

Pike Stave, Stock The shaft of a *pike (2).

Pilch A light frameless saddle for children; a rug or pad laid on a saddle. (Midlands)

Pild, Pilled Hemp Hemp from which the outer skin has been peeled.

Pill To strip bark from trees for use in tanning.

Pillar and Claw Table Table resting on a single pillar with a claw-shaped foot.

Pillion
1. Pad or small saddle attached to the rear of the main saddle, for a second rider or a *male (1).
2. Light saddle for a female rider.

Pillow Dish-shaped wooden block on which stone was placed for carving.

Pillow Bere, Cod Pillow case.

Pillow Tie Pillowcase. (Dor; Ham)

Pin Block Tool used by a currier. (Sal)

Pin Bouk Wooden bucket. (Dby)

Pin Wheel Device used in linen weaving. (Chs)

Pingle Small enclosure or paddock. (Dby)

Pinions
1. Short wool left in the comb after the long staple has been drawn off.
2. The skirt of a gown. (War)

Pinn Small cask holding half a firkin of 4½ gallons. (Dby; War)

Pinner
1. Officer who impounds stray animals in the pinfold.
2. A cap or neck-cloth; a *coif with two long flaps.

Pinsons Pincers.

Pint, Pinterpot Pint pot or measure; a drinking vessel.

Pintado Chintz: coloured cotton fabric often used for hangings or cloths.

Pipe A large cask used for wine, and also for other liquids and provisions; its capacity was 126 gallons, 2 hogsheads, or half a tun.

Pipkin Small eathenware (or, earlier, metal) pot or pan, round and deep, used in cooking.

Pirn The spool or bobbin on which thread is wound for the weft.

Piss Pot Chamber pot.

Pistol, Pistolet A small fire-arm, held and fired by one hand.

Pistol Bottle Bottle for carrying drink in one's pocket. (Hrt)

Pit Coal Coal from a pit, as opposed to charcoal.

Pit Grate Grating over a kitchen ash-pit.

Pitch *Hop Pitch.

Pitch Brand A distinctive mark of ownership on a sheep, made with pitch; the implement used to make the mark.

Pitch Skillet, Pan, Pot Pan for boiling tar to make pitch when branding sheep, or on board ship.

Placard Garment, often richly embroidered, worn beneath an open gown or coat.

Placebo Vespers in the office of the dead, from the first word in the Latin service.

Plaid Woollen cloth with a chequered pattern.

Plancherd, Planchin Boarding made of wooden planks; a floor or ceiling so made.

Plane
1. The shaft of a crossbow. (Oxf)
2. A type of woollen cloth. (Chs)

Plank Table Table top made of boards held together by battens, set up on trestles and taken down after use.

Plasher Hedge layer.

Plaster Curative substance spread on muslin and placed on the skin or wound.

Plat Chart or plan.

Plate Kitchen dishes of various kinds made from precious metals, i.e. gold and silver.

Plate Coat Leather corselet with small plates of iron sewn on.

Plate Ring Table mat to protect the table from hot plates.

Plate Warmer Plate with hollow bottoms for hot water, to keep it warm.

Plated Furniture overlaid with metal plates for ornamentation or protection.

Platter Flat dish of pewter, wood, or earthenware to hold food. Wooden platters were usually made of sycamore, they were always round, and thinner than trenchers.

Playing Table Table for games such as chess, backgammon, and cards, perhaps with the appropriate markings.

Pleache Hedging implement, designed to partly cut stems so that they could be bent down in order to make the hedge thicker; the cut stems would send up vertical shoots and thus renew the hedge.

Pleck Small piece of ground, a plot, a small enclosure.

Pledge Surety; anything handed over to another as security for performance of an agreement, *etc.*

Plitch Thick hempen material. (Dev)

Plock Blocks of sawn wood, sometimes also roots and stumps. (Gls)

Plough Beam A long, curved timber or iron beam, the main part of a plough, to which all the principal parts are attached.

Plough Gear, Stuff The harness, equipment and fittings of a plough.

Plough Irons The *coulter, *plough share, and any other iron parts of a plough.

Plough Share The pointed blade of a plough, which, following the *coulter, cuts the ground horizontally at the base of the furrow.

Plough Slip Metal plate with two metal strips underneath, acting as a sledge to haul the plough from field to farmstead. (Dby)

Plough String One of the traces of a plough.

Plough Timber All parts of the plough which were made of wood.

Plow Wagon. (Dor)

Plough Chain *Chain (1).

Plough Stilt Handle of a plough. (Northern)

Ploughbote The right to wood or timber for the construction and maintainance of a plough and other agricultural implements; a right normally enjoyed by tenants.

Plump
1. Pump.
2. Small, vertical butter churn. (Dor)

Plush Rich cloth with a long nap used in garments such as footmen's liveries, and in saddlery and upholstery.

Poatestone Sharpening stone for tools. (Gls)

Pocket A measure of hops; 1¼ hundredweight; sack or bag holding this amount.

Poddinger *Porringer.

Point Maker Maker of *points.

Point
1. Tagged lace or cord for lacing up clothes, e.g. attaching the *hose to a *doublet.
2. Needle.

Poite, Poyt Poker. (Dby; Yks)

Poitrel Breast plate for a horse.

Poke
1. A bag or small sack, especially one for carrying grain, *etc.,* on a pack saddle.
2. A device to prevent animals breaking through fences. (Dur)

Poke Cloth Sack cloth.

Poldavis Coarse sacking or canvas frequently used for sail cloth; originally from Poldavide in Brittany.

Pole
1. Stake.
2. Long handle of a scythe.
3. Long pole used in dyeing.

Pole Axe
1. Battle axe with a long handle; a *halberd.
2. Butchers axe for slaughtering, with a hammer on the opposite side to the blade.

Polke Cupboard. (Dur)

Pollenger Timber from pollarded trees, i.e. branches which have grown from stumps.

Pomander Small receptacle or necklace containing an aromatic substance to scent the air and ward off infection.

Pomet Lace Type of silk lace.

Pompillion *Populeon.

Poniard A dagger.

Poor Mens Box Box for alms in the church.

Poppinjay Fabric originally made in Poperinghe, in the Netherlands. (Wor)

Populeon Ointment made from the buds of the black poplar.

Porket A small or young pig.

Porr A fire poker. (Dur)

Porringer A bowl-shaped pewter or earthenware dish (or perhaps silver in wealthier households), often with a cover and ear-shaped handles, for porridge, soup, *potage, etc.*

Portal Partition or fixed screen within the door of a room to keep out draughts, made of *wainscot.

Portas, Porteous A portable breviary or prayer.

Portmanteau Trunk case or bag for storage of clothes or for carrying them when travelling.

Posnet
1. Small pot with a long handle and three short legs, used for boiling.
2. *Porringer.

Posset Drink of hot milk curdled with ale, vinegar, or wine, perhaps mixed with spices or sugar, drunk as a delicacy or as a cure for colds.

Posted Bedstead Bed with a canopy or *tester supported on four posts.

Pot Round cooking vessel, deep rather than broad, and with three feet, to stand or hang over the fire.

Pot Brass Alloy from which pots were made.

Pot Crooks, Gails, Hooks *Crook.

Pot Hanger *Hangings (1).

Pot Hangle *Hangles

Pot Kilp Moveable hook or handle for hanging pots over the fire. (Northern)

Pot Links The chain on which a *pot was suspended over the fire.

Pot Metal Alloy of lead and copper used to make pots.

Potage Thick soup, oatmeal, porridge, broth, *etc.*

Potash Pottassium carbonate, used in finishing woollen cloth, and for making soap.

Potgayle Hook suspended from a bar to hang pots over the fire.

Potter Poker. (Lan)

Pottinger *Porringer.

Pottle Measure of two quarts.

Pottle Pan, Pot A pot or tankard holding a *pottle; a drinking vessel.

Pouder *Pewter.

Pounced Metalwork that has been ornamentally embossed or chased.

Pouncet Box Box to hold sand for drying ink, or perhaps for perfume.

Pound A large trough used for crushing apples in cider-making. (Dev; Con)

Pounder Pestle; instrument for pounding.

Powder Blue Powdered smalt, used to whiten linen in the laundry.

Powder Horn A flask for gun powder, made from the horn of an ox or cow, with a metal or wooden covering.

Powdering Trough, Tub Salting or pickling tub for preserving meat with salt and spice.

Powger *Porringer.

Pown House Cider barn. (Dev)

Pows, Powltes Pulses (peas and beans).

Praised Appraised, i.e. priced or valued

Praisor The persons who listed and valued the goods in a probate inventory; the *appraiser.

Prechel Tool for punching holes in horse-shoes. (War)

Preculae The beads of a rosary. (Latin)

Presents The document being read.

Press
1. Large cupboard, with doors, and usually with shelves, for storing clothes, linen, books, *etc.,* sometimes placed in a wall recess. Often the top portion is recessed.
2. *Cheese Press.

Press Bedstead Bed that folds up into the shape of a *press(1) when not in use.

Press Board
1. Ironing Board. (Ham)
2. Table with a cupboard beneath. (Dby)

Press Cupboard Wardrobe in which clothes could be hung.

Pressing Iron Smoothing iron, for ironing clothes.

Prick Song Music 'pricked', i.e. written and sung from the script, rather than by ear or memory.

Pricket Spike for impaling a candlestick.

Prig Small pot or pan of brass or tin. (Yks)

Primella *Prunella.

Primer
1. Devotional manual or prayer book for use of the laity.
2. Elementary reading book.

Primer Seisen The right of the crown to receive from the heir of a tenant in chief the first year's income from his estate.

Principal
1. *Mortuary.
2. Main beams and supporting posts of a building.

Print Mould.

Pritchel Sharply pointed tool for punching holes; especially used by cobblers, and for punching nail-holes in horse-shoes.

Privy Stool *Close Barrell.

Processional Book containing litanies, hymns, *etc.,* for use in processions.

Proctor Lawyer who manages causes in a court of civil or canon law.

Prospective Glass
1. Magic glass for seeing the future.
2. Telescope.

Provender Chest Chest for storing animal feed, kept in a barn or stable.

Prow Lip, spout, or pointed projections.

Provision Stock or store of food.

Pruce Chest Either made of *spruce from Scandinavia, or imported from Prussia.

Prunella Strong material, originally silk, later worsted; used for the gowns of clergymen, lawyers and graduates.

Pug A six-month old lamb, or a ewe in its second year. (Bdf)

Puke Superior type of woollen cloth for making gowns; their bluish-black colour.

Pull Tow Hemp or tow not worth spinning; the coarse and knotty parts; its refuse. (Sfk)

Pullen Poultry; domestic fowl.

Puller Loft for poultry.

Pulse The edible seeds of leguminous crops such as peas, beans, and vetches, *etc.;* the plants themselves.

Pummice Stone Used to smooth the surface of parchment.

Pumping Tool Pump drills for drilling stone and metal; they operated with a pumping action. (Gls)

Punch A tool for indenting, piercing, or forcing bolts out of holes.

Punch Wood Wood used for joists, and for the upright timbers of wooden partitions.

Puncheon
1. *Punch.
2. A dagger.
3. *Pancheon.
4. Basket or cask for holding eels.

Pure Cloth trimmed or cut down to show one colour only.

Purfle A border, especially of a garment or cloth embroidered with gold or silver thread, and/or trimmed with pearls, fur, *etc.*

Purgatory Receptacle for ashes placed beneath or in front of the fire, which could be used as a milder source of heat than the fire itself. (Sal; Wor)

Purl Twisted gold or silver thread, used in bordering and embroidery; the loops or twists made by this thread on embroidered cloth.

Purlin A beam (usually one of two or more) running along the length of a roof, resting on the principal rafters, which it crosses at right angles, and supporting common rafters.

Purr Poker. (Dby)

Put to use Invest.

Putcheon *Puncheon (4)

Puter, Putor, Putter *Pewter.

Putt
1. Heavy two-wheeled cart, made to tip. (Dev; Dor)
2. A cask.

Pux *Pug.

Q

Quarrell, Quarry
1. Diamond-shaped or square pane of glass used in *lattice windows.
2. A short heavy square-arrow for a cross-bow.

Quart A measure of capacity: a quarter of a *gallon or two pints; a pot holding this amount.

Quarter
1. A square panel.
2. The skirt of a coat or other garment. (Oxf)
3. A measure of capacity of grain, eight bushels, but varying by locality.

Quarter Vessell Containing 25 gallons of liquid. (Wor)

Quartern A quarter of various weights and measures.

Queell Twill; the warp.

Queeling Turn Device for winding the warp.

Queens Ware Pale cream-coloured earthenware, originally made by Wedgwood and so-called due to the patronage of Queen Charlotte.

Quern Small stone hand mill for grinding grain, malt, mustard, *etc.* It consisted of two circular stones, rotated one on top of the other.

Quern House Room for milling.

Quick Goods, Stuff Live animals.

Quill A spool on which the weft is wound for placing in the shuttle.

Quill Gold Gold thread.

Quill Torn, Wheel The spool of a spinning wheel, on which the weft is wound so that it can be placed in the shuttle.

Quillet A small plot or strip of land.

Quilt Made up of a layer of wool, flock, feathers, *etc.,* between two large pieces of material, stitched together. Originally used to lie on, but subsequently as a bed covering.

Quilted Coat Armoured jacket worn by infantry.

Quilting Frame Frame on which a counterpane is stretched in the process of quilting.

Quire Four sheets of paper or parchment folded to form eight leaves; a small book.

Quiver A case for holding arrows.

Quoin Wedge shaped block used for various purposes.

Quy Heifer or female calf up to three years old, or before it has calved. (Northern)

Quystirk Heifer of one to two years. (Ntt)

R

Rack
1. An iron bar supporting a spit or cooking utensils.
2. A wooden or metal frame holding animal fodder, which may be in a stable, *etc.,* or in a field.
3. *Tenter.
4. Support for a cross-bow.
5. Framework for storing plates, *etc.*

Rackan A chain or *rack (1) supporting a pot over the fire.

Rackan Crook, Hook, Team, Tree Ratcheted iron hook, bar or crane in the chimney, from which *rackans and *pot crooks could be suspended.

Raded, Radden Made of wattle.

Raddle The *laths used in wattle and daub buildings.

Radlings Slender rods, usually of hazel, fastened between upright stakes to form a wall or partition.

Raff Imported timber, usually in the form of *deal.

Raffle Wooden instrument used to stir blazing brushwood whilst it was heating an oven. (Nfk)

Ragot Of variegated design and pattern; patchwork. (Gls)

Raid *Rave.

Rail
1. A garment: a woman's *neckerchief, shoulder cape, cloak, or jacket.
2. *Rave.

Raiment Clothing; *apparel.

Rainer Fine linen made in Rennes, Brittany.

Raised Work Cloth that has been embossed, or on which a pattern has been cut in the pile.

Rait
1. *Rave.

2. The process of watering hemp or flax by placing it on ' raitles', i.e. racks, in a pond or ditch for some time. (Chs)

Rammel Brushwood, underwood, *etc.,* especially from trees that have been felled; rubbish. (Northern)

Rammill Skimmed milk. (Dor)

Randing Knife For cutting meat into strips. (Gls)

Range. Ranger
1. An iron fire grate, especially one with one or two ovens at its side.
2. Sieve or strainer.

Rape A crop grown for oil seed.

Rapier A long, pointed two-edged sword, chiefly designed for thrusting; a small, light sword.

Rash A smooth fabric made of silk or worsted.

Rasp A coarse file, with teeth raised on its surface by means of a pointed punch.

Rat Coloured Dull grey, as used in funeral gowns.

Rat Snatch, Stock Rat trap.

Rate A local tax, especially for the church or the poor.

Rath *Rave.

Ratles Part of a loom. (Dur)

Ratsbane Rat poison, especially arsenic.

Rave
1. Rails, framework or shelving which may be attached to the side of a cart to enable a greater load to be carried.
2. The bar on a loom, fitted with teeth, which guides the warp as it is being wound on the beam.

Ream Twenty quires, or 480 sheets of paper.

Ream Pot Cream pot.

Reamer Vat in which curd is set to harden into cheese.

Reap Hook Scythe with a curved steel blade and a serrated edge, about eighteen inches long.

Reasons of the Sun Raisins; sun-dried grapes.

Red Ochre An earth much used as a pigment; it consisted of a mixture of hydrated oxide of iron and clay.

Red Sanders Wood of the East Indies; red sandalwood or rubywood tree, used in dyeing and for medicinal purposes.

Red Wheat A variety of wheat, reddish in colour.

Red Wood Generic name for the different types of wood from which various red dyes were extracted.

Reddle Red ochre for marking sheep.

Reed
1. Wheat straw for thatching.
2. That part of a loom through which warp threads pass.

Reed Wrought Chair Rush bottomed and backed chair.

Reeing Sieve Fine sieve of brass or iron, for riddling and cleansing corn.

Reel
1. A framework for winding yarn; the spool of a spinning wheel; sometimes the spinning wheel itself, or a device for spinning without a wheel.
2. A plumb-line or measuring string. (Gls)

Release A deed conveying property.

Relict Widow.

Reliquary Receptacle for the relics of saints, i.e. their bones.

Remainder The residual interest in an estate, usually after the death of its occupier, created by the same conveyance by which the latter came into possession.

Remland, Remlet, Renling Remainder, residue.

Rennet Pot Pot to hold rennet, used in cheese-making.

Rep Fabric of wood, silk or cotton, with a corded surface.

Reparrell, Reppell *Apparell.

Requiem Mass said or sung for the repose of the souls of the dead, from the first word of the Latin introit.

Rere Dorter Area in a monastery behind the *dorter, often used for latrines.

Reredos
1. Ornamental screen of wood or stone covering the wall behind an altar; a curtain used for the same purpose.
2. The back of a brick or stone fireplace; an iron plate forming a fire back.

Rest, Rester A forked support for a musket used to steady the barrel when firing to ensure greater accuracy of fire; it had a spike to fix it in the ground.

Ret To soften hemp by soaking it in water, thus dis-engaging the fibres.

Ret Pit A pit in which flax or hemp was retted.

Reversion That part of an estate which reverts to the grantor or his representative after the term of the original grant has been completed.

Revolving Churn *Churn.

Rew The ridge into which grass falls when cut with a scythe.

Rewer Rake used to make *rews.

Rial A gold coin, either Spanish or English, originally worth about ten shillings. First issued in England by Edward IV in 1465.

Rick A stack of hay, wood, corn, *etc.,* especially one that has been thatched to keep it dry.

Rick Barton Enclosure for hay ricks; farmyard.

Rick Staddle, Stavel Frame of wood placed on *staddle stones or oak posts, on which ricks were built.

Riddle Large, coarse-meshed sieve for separating seed from corn.

Rider Piece of wood with which a pair of harrows is connected.

Ridgarth Type of horse girth. (Chs)

Ridge, Rigg *Selion or strip of arable in the open field.

Ridgel, Rigeld An imperfectly castrated animal, or one whose genitals are not perfectly developed.

Riding Beast Horse.

Riffler Implement for breaking up rough ground where a plough cannot go.

Rig Ridge in a ploughed field where sheaves of corn were placed after harvesting.

Rigell Cloth-making tool. (Dev)

Rigged Cow with a white stripe on its back.

Ring
1. Cider press.
2. Table mat.
3. Circular pewter plate.
4. Part of a horse's harness.

Ring Bittle *Beetle with an iron ring around its head.

Ring House Room or building housing a cider press.

Ringer One who rings church bells; probate records frequently refer to funeral ringers.

Rip Hook Reaping hook; scythe with a curved steel blade about 18" long, having a serrated edge.

Ripple
1. *Rave. (Sal)
2. *Rippling Comb.
3. The iron rim on a cart wheel. (Sal)

Rippling Comb, Stock Instrument toothed like a comb, used to separate seeds from flax or hemp.

Road Saddle Riding saddle.

Roan Horse of mixed colour, in which red predominates.

Roan Hood Hood made with linen from Rouen.

Roasting Iron *Gridiron used especially for roasting eggs.

Rock, Roke *Distaff, perhaps with the wool or flax attached to it.

Rock Tree The long handle by which a blacksmith worked his bellows.

Roll
1. *Bederoll.
2. Pad to facilitate the carrying of heavy loads, e.g. pails of milk, on the head.

Romble *Rammel.

Rombowline Poor quality rope or canvas used by seamen for temporary purposes.

Rome Piece of land. (Dur)

Rood
1. A measure of land area, containing 40 square poles or perches, but varying in different regions.
2. Crucifix, especially one above the screen between the chancel and the nave.

Rood Loft Loft or gallery above the rood screen in a church upon which the *rood or cross was mounted; also used for an attic in a large house.

Roof Meat *Flitches, often hung from the roof.

Rook A heap, stack, or small pile, especially of stones, turf, *etc*. (Northern)

Rosa Solis A cordial or liquor, originally made from the juice of the sundew plant, later from spirits and spices.

Rose Nail Wrought iron nail with a round head facetted by a series of hammer blows, used to secure iron fittings.

Roset Rose-coloured pigment; a distillation from roses.

Rose Water Water distilled from roses and used as a perfume.

Rosil Resin.

Rosin
1. Cobblers wax. (Dur)
2. Adhesive derived from trees. (Lin)

Rother Horned cattle; an ox.

Rotten Stone A decomposed siliceous limestone found in the Peak District, used as a powder for polishing metals, *etc.*

Rough
1. Roof. (Con)
2. Raw, i.e. referring to meat. (Wor)

Round
1. A quantity of material rolled up.
2. A single turn of yarn wound on a reel.
3. A round wooden *trencher.

Round Cloth Canvas.

Roundabout Chair Lavishly ornamented chairs with cane-work seats, semi-circular backs and cabriole legs, originally imported from the East Indies via Holland.

Roundel Ring or hoop holding candles, to hang before a rood or image.

Rove, Roving Raw, untwisted thread; partially spun worsted.

Rowel The small wheel with spikes on spurs.

Rowen Refuse after threshing. (Gls)

Rowle
1. A measure of lard. (Chs)
2. *Rowler.

Rowler
1. Rolling pin.
2. Horse roller, used to crush clods and smooth the ground.

Rowling Stone Stone *rowler (2).

Rowling Hose Stockings, the tops of which may be rolled up or down.

Rubber A hand brush, cloth, *etc.,* used for cleaning and polishing.

Rubber File Tool for taking the scale off red-hot iron. (Sal)

Ruck Heap or stack of coal or other fuel.

Rudder
1. *Rother

2. Coarse sieve.
3. Paddle-like utensil for stirring the malt in the *mashing fat.

Rue Oil Oil extracted from the rue plant for medicinal purposes.

Ruff, Ruffle Starched linen frill for neck and wrist wear, crimped or fluted extravagantly, worn by both sexes, but only by the wealthy.

Rug
1. Coverlet (where the word is used in conjunction with other bed-linen).
2. A rough woollen material similar to *frieze.

Rugged Shaggy, rough with hair.

Run Bed *Truckle Bed.

Run Net Net which can be run out in a continuous stretch. (Lin)

Runlet
1. Small cask for wine, or for holding the *wort whilst brewing
2. Circular wooden trencher.

Runnel A small water-course: a ditch, gutter or small stream.

Running Glass Hour glass.

Running Tub Tub for rennet.

Runt Oxen Small breed of oxen; oxen of poor quality.

Rushia Chair Chairs, either (1) with rush seats, or (2) from Russia, upholstered in *Russia leather.

Russell A ribbed or corded woollen fabric, probably of Flemish origin.

Russet Coarse home-spun woollen cloth, usually of a reddish-brown colour, used by country people for clothing; the colour itself.

Russia Leather Durable, light leather, made from skins cured using oil derived from birch bark, and often used for book bindings.

S

Sack
1. Cloth often used for window covering.
2. A bag made of coarse flax or hemp for the storage of dry goods; a measure of the quantity of goods, e.g. hops, corn, flour, *etc.*
3. Dry white wine imported from Spain and the Canaries.

Sack Cloth A coarse fabric used for making bags and sacks.

Sad
1. Dull or dark; a sombre colour.
2. In relation to metal-ware, solid, dense, heavy.

Sad Iron A solid smoothing iron, for ironing cloth.

Sad Ware Heavy or dark-coloured goods, especially metalware such as pots, chargers, fire backs, *etc.*

Saddle Tree Framework of a saddle; the block on which it was shaped.

Safe Food cupboard, or chest, with sides of woven hair allowing ventilation, but keeping out flies and other insects: an *aumbry.

Safeguard Outer skirt or petticoat, worn by women over their kirtle as a protection against dirt when riding.

Sagathy Woollen worsted fabric.

Sage *Swage.

Sage Cheese Cheese flavoured and mottled by liquid pressed from sage leaves.

Sag Chair Rush seated chair, i.e. sedge.

Salamander Circular iron plate attached to a long handle, placed in a fire until red hot, then used to brown pastry, omelettes, *etc.*

Sallet
1. A close-fitting armoured helmet with a protective backpiece, and perhaps with a vizor, made of steel.
2. An iron vessel.
3. A salad dish.

Saloon The principal reception room in a gentleman's house.

Salt, Salt Pie, Pitch A container or box for salt and other condiments; a salt cellar, or perhaps a block of salt.

Salt Box, Cote, House Box or room for storing salt, or perhaps the place where it is produced.

Salt Victuals Meat salted for preservation.

Salter Psalter, i.e. the book of Psalms.

Salting Bench, Cowl, Kimnel, Store, Trough, Tub Bench, *kimnel, *cowl (2), trough or tub used for salting meat or fish.

Salvatory Box to hold ointments.

Salver A broad flat piece of plate, usually with a foot, used as a tray.

Sameron Cloth with a texture between linen and hemp. (Dur; Yks)

Samphire Plant with fleshy leaves used in pickles.

Sampler Piece of embroidered canvas.

Sand Box Box with a perforated lid used to sprinkle sand on wet ink as a blotter to dry it.

Sand Sack Sack for carrying sand from the beach to use as fertilizer. (Con)

Sandalwood, Sanders A scented wood rendering a yellow or red dye; *red sanders.

Sandaric Red arsenic sulphide.

Sandiver Saline liquid found on glass after vitrification; glass gall.

Sap Type of spade or mattock.

Sap Lath A *lath made of sapwood.

Sarch *Searce (1).

Sarcophagus Piece of equipment, e.g. a wine cooler, a grate, in the shape of an Egyptian sarcophagus.

Sarpe Collar or neck ring of gold or silver.

Sarplier A large canvas sack for wool or other merchandise, containing 80 tods.

Sarsaparilla Tonic derived from the dried roots of a South American tree.

Sarsenet A very fine soft silk, used for quilts, linings, bed *hangings, *etc.*

Sasafras Dried bark of a North American tree, used medicinally.

Sash Line Sash cord for opening and closing windows; sash windows were introduced at the end of the 17th century.

Satin Silk fabric with a glossy surface on one side.

Satinisco An inferior quality satin.

Saucepan Small *skillet, with a long handle, for boiling sauces.

Saucer Sauceboat, usually metal, used for holding sauces and condiments; they were not used to hold cups until the 18th century.

Saunders *Sandalwood

Save All Candlestick used for burning candle ends.

Saving Iron
1. Iron plate or fender to protect the coal from the heat of the fire. (Dev)
2. Dripping pan. (Dev)

Say
1. Fine cloth, similar to serge, formerly partly of silk, but subsequently entirely woollen, and used for bedding and wall hangings, table coverings, *etc.*
2. Bucket with two ears, through which a pole may be passed to make a handle for one or two to carry.

Scabbard Sheath or case for a sword, protecting the blade.

Scabellum Stool or bench. (Latin)

Scaffold *Staddle

Scala Caeli Chapel or altar to which an indulgence was attached; originally the name of a church near Rome to which the same indulgence was attached.

Scalding Tub Early form of sterilizer for cleansing utensils, especially those used in the dairy.

Scale Baulk The bar of a balance.

Scallop In the shape of a shell.

Scammony Gum resin from convovulus roots, used as a strong purgative.

Scamnum A bench. (Latin)

Scavilones Long drawers worn under the *hose by men.

Scellett, Scillett *Skillet

Scia The sleeve-opening of a gown. (Dur)

Scoath Pole, bar or forked stick. (Dur)

Scollop Rod used to fasten down thatch on roofs: a thatch peg.

Scomer *Skimmer

Sconce
1. Candle holder, perhaps fitted to a wall, and perhaps with a screen to protect the flame. In wealthy households it would have a polished backplate or mirror to reflect the light.
2. Screen, partition, seat or stone shelf in the kitchen.
3. Kitchen utensil set before the fire.

Sconce Glass Looking glass fitted with sockets to hold candles.

Scoop Joint of mutton or beef. (Dev)

Scoot Small piece of ground, the corner of a field.

Scotch Cap Head gear made of thick woollen cloth, without a brim, decorated with tails or streamers.

Scotch Cloth Linen supposedly woven with nettle fibres: cheap fabric resembling *lawn.

Scraw
1. A scroll or tag of parchment or leather.
2. Frame on which fabric is hung to dry.

Screel
1. Wooden bucket or tub for holding water or milk. (Lin)
2. Screen for dressing corn. (Lin; Yks)

Screen
1. A moveable partition, perhaps for stopping draughts, or for protection from the heat of a fire.
2. A *settle. (Lan)
3. A wire sieve on a frame, used to separate grain from chaff, dust and other impurities.
4. A marking iron. (Dev)
5. A cloth-making tool. (Dev)

Screen Mill Apparatus for sifting malt. (Dev)

Screw Plate A hardened steel plate used by smiths to cut screw threads; it has tapped holes of various diameters drilled in it.

Screw Press Press such as a cyder or cheese press, operated by a screw.

Scribbling The first stage in the treatment of fleece wool, in which the fibres are straightened before carding begins.

Scriptor Bureau or desk with shelves for books, and drawers; an *escritoire.

Scrivenor A *notary or copyist; one who drafts or copies documents such as wills, *bonds, deeds, etc.

Scull *Skull.

Scullery Small back kitchen.

Scummer *Skimmer.

Scuppet Broad wooden shovel often made from willow, used by maltsters and hop driers.

Scutcheon *Escutcheon.

Scuttle Winnowing implement; either a wicker basket or a bowl, in which the grain could be agitated, or a shovel to toss it in the air, so that the wind could separate the wheat from the chaff.

Sea Card Marine chart.

Sea Coal Coal. The name is usually explained by the fact that London was supplied with coal by sea from Newcastle upon Tyne. But not all sea coal was carried by sea, and this explanation has been questioned.

Seal Rope or chain for tying animals up. (Nfk)

Sealed, Sealing
1. Walls which have been lined or overlaid with panelling or *wainscot.
2. Rooms which have had a ceiling installed, hiding the rafters, and perhaps covering the floor boards of an upper storey.
3. Furniture such as beds and chairs which are panelled, with a solid frame.

Seam
1. A packhorse load or cartload.
2. A measure of corn.
3. Fat, grease, hogs lard.

Seaman's Needle Compass.

Seam Pannier Basket for carrying fat or grease.

Seaming Lace Lace inserted into, or covering and ornamenting, seams in clothing or fabric.

Seamster One engaged in fine sewing for a livelihood.

Searce, Search
1. A fine sieve, which might be made of sheepskin in which small holes had been drilled, and used for sifting flour; alternatively, it might be made of bristles or cloth and used in the dairy.
2. A tool for nicking wrought iron or steel. (Sal)

Seat
1. A piece of leather forming the foundation for a heel in boots and shoes.
2. A pillion for a woman, fastened behind the saddle.
3. A blacksmiths tool used for cutting iron.

Seblet *Seedlip.

Sedge Coarse grasses much used for making chairs, brushes, etc.

Seed Cod, Cot, Hope *Seedlip.

Seedlip A basket shaped to fit the waist, with a shoulder strap, used to carry seed when it is being sown.

Seeing Glass Looking glass or mirror.

Seeler Tapestry canopy or covering for a bed. (War)

Seg
1. *Sedge.
2. An animal which has been castrated when fully grown, e.g. a bull, a pig, a sheep.

Selion One of several parallel strips of land in an open field, lying between two furrows.

Sell A low seat or stool. (Ham)

Sellar *Cellar: a store room, not necessarily underground.

Seller of Bottles Case or stand for holding bottles.

Sellepp, Selliop *Seedlip.

Semmet Implement used in winnowing. (Dev)

Sempiternum Twilled woollen stuff, similar to *perpetuana.

Sendal Thin silken material.

Senvy Mustard seed.

Serge A woollen fabric, whose precise nature has varied over time. Originally it was used for *hangings (2), bed coverings, *etc.;* from the 16th century it was worn by the poorer classes on account of its durability; subsequently a durable, twilled worsted fabric.

Seron Bale of exotic products, e.g. almonds, cocoa, *etc.,* encased in an animal's hide.

Serpentine Type of cannon, often used as a ship's gun in the 15th and 16th centuries.

Serpentine Powder Gunpowder for use with a *serpentine.

Serrandole Type of candlestick or candelabra.

Serve A shallow basket used for a horse's feed. (Wor)

Sester A measure of beer or wine; a vessel for holding that measure.

Set
1. Jewellery set on a garment.
2. A squared stone used for paving.

3. Tool used as a punch for rivetting.
4. A large piece of coal.
5. Jack for lifting the *axletree of a wagon or carriage

Set Pot Iron cauldron set in stone or brick above a grate, used for boiling clothes.

Set Work Stitching or embroidery used in tapestry.

Seth Sieve or milk-strainer. (Dur)

Setter Net or trap for catching or killing birds.

Setting Net Net used for catching rabbits, hares, *etc.,* or a fishing net for setting across a stream.

Setting Stick
1. A stick used to make holes for 'setting' plants.
2. A rod used in making the pleats of *ruffs.

Settle
1. Long wooden bench, with a high back, arms, and cupboards underneath, capable of seating several people
2. Raised shelf or frame, of brick or wood, for supporting barrels or milk cans.

Settle Bed Bed which folds into a *settle (1).

Severalty Land held by one individual in a consolidated, enclosed area of land, as opposed to scattered strips in the open field held in common.

Sewstern *Cistern.

Shack Fork Wooden fork for shaking corn out of straw. (Dby)

Shackles
1. Iron links connecting the plough beam to the swingletree.
2. *Horse lock.

Shag Thick piled, long haired cloth, usually worsted, with a velvet nap on one side.

Shagreen Leather made from horse hide, dyed green, and used to cover small boxes and cases, *etc.*

Shalloon A closely woven woollen cloth often used for linings.

Shallop Sloop: a large, heavy boat, with one or more masts, and sometimes with guns.

Shamey Chamois: a soft pliable leather originally from the skin of the chamois (a species of antelope), but subsequently obtained from the skins of sheep, goats, deer, calves, *etc.*

Shank Fur obtained from the legs of animals, especially kids, goats, or sheep, used to trim outer garments.

Shank Pan Small pan with a long handle. (Dur)

Share
1. *Plough Share.
2. *Shears.

Shave Tool for smoothing or paring wood.

Sheal Husk of oats, wheat, *etc.*

Shear Board Padded board on which cloth was stretched for cropping with hand-shears.

Shear Wether Sheep after its first shearing.

Shearing Knife A broad bladed tool to cut the edges of thatch.

Shearman One who shears woollen cloth.

Shears A term applied to various implements resembling a large pair of scissors, e.g. for cutting cloth, for shearing sheep, *etc.*

Shed The opening of the warp threads through which the weft shuttle passes.

Sheder A lamb of 8 months plus, prior to its first shearing. (Lin; Yks)

Sheede, Sheedle Rough wooden implement or pole. (Dev)

Sheep Bar
1. Hurdles used for sheep folds.
2. *Sheep rack.

Sheep Mark Implement for making marks of ownership on sheep.

Sheep Rack
1. Hurdle on which sheep were held whilst being shorn.
2. A rack from which sheep feed.

Sheer
1. A crop of grass.
2. The quantity of wool cut from an entire flock in one season.
3. The part of a wagon to which the shafts are attached.
4. A sheath.
5. A *plough share.

Sheers
1. *Shears.
2. Coal tongs. (Gls)

Shelboard *Raves.

Sheorbo *Theorbo

Shield Board The mould board of a plough.

Sheppick Pitch fork with tines set widely apart and a short handle.

Shide A plank or thin board.

Shift The division of the open field with a view to rotating crops.

Shilling Silver coin worth twelve pence.

Ship In ecclesiastical contexts, a container for incense.

Shippon Cattle shed or cow house.

Shirt Band Shirt collar, *ruff, or wrist-band.

Shive
1. Bung for stopping casks.
2. Small iron wedge fastening the bolt of a window shutter.

Shod, Shoed Furnished with a shoe of metal, e.g. cart wheels rimmed with iron, shovels edged with metal, *etc.*

Shoeing The metal tyre of a wheel.

Shoeing Box Frame for controlling horses when being shod.

Shole, Showle Shovel.

Shoot
1. An open trough.
2. A litter of pigs.

Shooter Board placed between cheeses when in the press.

Shop The work-place of a craftsman; place where business was conducted.

Shop Board Table or counter on which business was transacted, or goods displayed.

Shop Book Account book for recording trading debts.

Shop Stuff Stock in trade.

Shot
1. Young pig that has been weaned.
2. An idle worthless youth.
3. Ill grown ewe; the animals left when the best of the flock have been selected.
4. A fabric with warp threads of one colour, and weft threads of another.

Shoull, Showle Shovel.

Shove Large fork used to pick up oats when harvesting.

Shovel Tree The handle of a spade or shovel.

Shrapnet Snare or trap for birds, baited with corn. (Ess)

Shredding Prunings or loppings of trees and undergrowth.

Shredden Heling Patchwork coverlet.

Shrine Box or coffer.

Shroud
1. The ropes attached to the top of a ship's mast.
2. Sheet in which a corpse is wrapped for burial.

Shruff Waste wood for the fire; also applied to old brass or copper.

Shuffleboard Table for a game in which a coin is driven by the blow of a hand across a highly polished surface, marked with transverse lines.

Shut
1. Bar or bolt to lock the door.
2. Shutter.

Shuttle Spool carrier in a weaver's loom; used for shuttling the *weft between the threads of the warp.

Side Bedstead A bedstead which fitted against the wall, and therefore had only two posts, rather than four.

Side Saddle Lady's saddle made so that both feet are on the same side of the horse.

Sideboard Table fixed against a wall, for eating, or for the display of household plate; later ones had cupboards and drawers, *etc.,* and the display function became more important.

Sie Boul Bowl to be used with a *searce (1) when straining liquids, especially milk.

Sile
1. *Sile Dish.
2. One of a pair of main timbers in a timber-framed house.

Sile Dish Wooden strainer with a linen bottom for straining milk.

Silk Frame Frame on which silk is stretched to be embroidered.

Sill *Thill (Dby; Yks)

Sillatory *Still (2). (War)

Silver Foin Silver hammered into thin sheets.

Silver Gilt Silver plated with a thin layer of gold.

Silver Stone
1. Jewellery set in silver.
2. Stoneware jug with a silver rim.

Sime Straw rope or cord holding down the thatch of hay stacks, *etc.* (Northern)

Simnel Bread or bun made from fine flour; a rich currant cake, traditionally eaten on the mid-Sunday in Lent.

Simple Pot A pot for *simples or medicines.

Simple Medicine.

Sink Stone Stone basin in a kitchen with a pipe attached, where dishes were washed, and where water could drain away.

Sinker Circular lid of a *cheese press, which presses the curds down to form the cheese. (Northern)

Sippets Small chunks of bread, perhaps toasted or fried, eaten with soup or *posset.

Sisers Scissors. (Dev)

Sisters Thread Bleached thread.

Sithorne *Cithern.

Sivet, Sivil Square iron bar or buckle beside a *saddle tree, on which to hang girth straps or stirrup leathers.

Skale Wooden cup or goblet. (Dby)

Skeel Wooden tub or bucket for milk or water; the handles were formed by staves projecting above the rim.

Skelboose, Skelbuse Front boards of a cow stall. (Lin; Yks)

Skele Dish or platter. (War)

Skelf Shelf. (Dur)

Skellat A small hand bell, used for ecclesiastical purposes, or by a bell-man. (Lin)

Skene Knife or dagger.

Skep
1. Beehive made of straw.
2. Basket or hamper for grain or coal.
3. Bowl-shaped vessel with handles for ladling.

Skeining Wheel Wheel for winding wool into skeins.

Skey One of a pair of wooden bars at each end of an ox-yoke, to which the neck-straps are attached. (Dur)

Skeys of Sherops Cloth-making tools. (Dev)

Skile Thin, shallow vessel for skimming milk. (Lin)

Skillet
1. A metal pan with three or four short legs and a long handle, used for boiling or stewing over an open fire; a large *posnet.
2. A pan without legs, similar to a frying pan or sauce pan, and made of brass or copper. (Sal)

Skimmer
1. Flat perforated metal ladle for removing scum or fat from boiling liquids, or for skimming cream from milk; a cooking ladle.
2. Fire shovel or scoop for raking ashes.

Skin Wool Wool from the skin of a dead sheep.

Skip
1. *Skep (2).
2. Small utensil for taking up yeast.
3. A child's long gown.

Skiver Skewer, used to fasten meat together whilst being cooked.

Skull A close fitting armoured helmet.

Slab Board Rough sap-wood plank with bark on one side, cut from a log when it was first squared up.

Slat Narrow strip of wood or stone used for roofing.

Slaughter Cradle Pen in which animals were slaughtered.

Slay, Sley The wooden frame holding the reed and driving home the weft; the handboard of a loom.

Slay Silk Silk thread for embroidery, which can be separated into smaller filaments.

Sled, Sledge
1. A flat bottomed truck which slid over the ground, used for transporting heavy goods; often used in harvesting on steep slopes, where a low centre of gravity was essential, or for transporting ploughs.
2. Sledge hammer used by blacksmiths for beating iron on an anvil.

Sled Bridle Harness for a *sled.

Sleeper Wooden beam used as a support for a wall or floor, *etc.* in a building.

Slice
1. Collective term for a variety of flattish cooking utensils, e.g. a spatula.
2. Fire shovel, used particularly for taking ashes out of bread ovens. Its end was shaped like a spade or paddle.

Sling Trace The chains or ropes connecting the horse's collar to the *swingletree.

Slip
1. Spoon handle with its top cut off obliquely.
2. A measure of yarn.
3. A young pig.

Slip Sconce A long or elongated *sconce.

Slipping Large skein of spun thread or yarn.

Slivered Wool A continuous strand of wool in a loose, untwisted condition, ready for *slubbing preparatory to spinning.

Slob Bench Working surface for use when handling liquids. (Sal)

Slubbing Removing lumpy imperfections from *slivered wool.

Small Beer Beer of a weak or inferior quality.

Smiths Coal
1. Charcoal.
2. *Coal.

Smock
1. A woman's undergarment; a shift.
2. A man's loose outer garment, worn by farm labourers instead of a coat, and reaching the knees.

Smoke Jack Fan in a flue, which revolved in the rising smoke, and powered a revolving spit; see *jack (1).

Smoothing Box *Ironing Box.

Smoothing Iron Implement for ironing clothes.

Snaffle A simple form of bridle bit, without a curb.

Snath, Snead Crooked shaft or handle of a scythe.

Snett Deer fat. (Ess)

Snip Horse with a white patch on its nostril or lip.

Snuffer Scissors for snuffing out candles and trimming their wicks, with a closed box to hold the charred wick.

Snype Poor, boggy pasture. (Dur)

Soa, Soe Large round tub for brewing, or washing clothes in. Not to be confused with sow, i.e. female pig.

Soale *Plough share. (Dev)

Sock *Plough share

Soe
1. *Say (2).
2. *Soa.

Soil Human excrement used as manure.

Solar An upper room, or loft often with a large window to catch the sunlight.

Soling Leather Leather for making shoe soles.

Sommer *Sumpter horse.

Sore *Sorrel (1).

Sorrel
1. Bright chestnut colour; often a horse of this colour.
2. Herb used in salads and cookery, or as a medicine.

Sorry Decrepit, old, of little value, poor.

Soul Scot Payment due to the church on the death of a person; a *mortuary.

Sow
1. Female pig.
2. Bar or ingot of some metal.
3. Mould for cast iron.

Sowel
1. A plough with a sole to which the share is attached.
2. Hurdle stake. (Dor)

Sowl A wash tub.

Spaning Calf, Pig Weaning calf or pig. (Ntt; Yks)

Spanish Brown Type of earth yielding a reddish-brown pigment.

Spanish Money Foreign coins circulated widely in England in the early modern period.

Spanish Table Portable table that folds up.

Spar
1. A thatching rod, made of split willow, pointed and twisted double.
2. A piece of timber, perhaps a rafter, or a large bolt for a door.

Sparable, Sparrow Bill Small, headless, wedge-shaped nail used in shoe-making.

Spark Fragment; remnant.

Sparver A canopy for a bed or cradle.

Spatter Spatula.

Spatterdash, Splatterdash Long cloth, leather leggings, or gaiters, to prevent trousers or stockings being spattered with dirt when riding.

Spattle Staff The handle of a spade.

Speak Piece of wood used to keep thatch in place.

Specet *Specialty.

Specialty A sealed *bond or *obligation, often entered into as security for a loan or debt.

Specie Coin; coined money.

Speer Wooden framed screen on the inside of a door or by the fire to keep out draughts; if made of wainscot they were termed *portals. On the inside, a *settle and a shelf might be attached.

Spence A service room: a pantry, larder, buttery, *etc.,* or perhaps a cupboard or a container for milk.

Sperate Debt Debt likely to be recovered, perhaps under a *specialty or *obligation.

Spermaceti A fatty substance derived from sperm whale, used to make candles, and for medicinal purposes.

Spialty *Specet.

Spigot, Spile, Spill Wooden stopper for the vent-hole of a cask or barrel.

Spill Part of a plough. (Dev)

Spill Press Press for finishing cloth, using 'spills' i.e. interleaved paper. (Dev)

Spill Wood Wood refuse 'spilt' by sawyers.

Spindle The earliest hand device for spinning wool, which puts the twist in the yarn and carries it round on its shank.

Spindle Chair Arm chair made mainly of spindles, i.e. cylindrical wooden bars.

Spindle Whorl The small round weight at the lower end of a *spindle which acted as a fly-wheel.

Spinning Turn *Turn (1).

Spinked Speckled, spotted. (Yks)

Spinet A keyed musical instrument, similar to a harpsichord, but smaller and single-stringed.

Spinning Spun thread or yarn.

Spinster A woman who spins, especially one whose usual occupation this is; not necessarily a single woman.

Spire *Portal. (Oxf)

Spit A thin revolving bar thrust through meat and stood on *cobirons in front of the open fire, for roasting.

Spittle Spade Small spade.

Spitting Sheet Small sheet of linen at the bedside for spitting into.

Spitting Tub, Box Spittoon; receptacle for spit, usually round and flat, of earthenware or metal and sometimes with a cover in the shape of a funnel.

Splints Flexible armour made of small overlapping plates to protect the arms and elbows.

Splot Plot or small piece of land.

Spokeshave A small plane, with slightly curved blade, used by carpenters, coopers, wheel-wrights, *etc.,* to shape barrel staves, spokes, *etc.*

Spoking Chain Used to fit spokes to a wheel.

Sponge
1. Long narrow strip of enclosed land. (Sfk)
2. Ground of a swampy or boggy nature.

Spooling Swift A light reel on which a skein of silk is placed to be wound off. (Oxf)

Spoon Mould Tinker's mould for making spoons.

Sprigged Cloth patterned with flowers or leaves, which might be embroidered, woven, or stamped; also applied to ceramic ware.

Spring
1. A copse or wood where young trees are growing from old stools.
2. A plantation, especially one enclosed for keeping game.

Spring Saw A bow saw.

Spring Tree *Swingletree.

Sprit Nautical term for a small boom or pole which crosses the sail of a boat diagonally from the mast to the upper corner of the sail.

Spruce Goods imported from Prussia and the Baltic, especially spruce leather, used for making jerkins; spruce fir, often used for making coffers and boxes, *etc.;* spruce ochre, a yellow or orange-brown pigment.

Spud A digging implement with a narrow chisel-shaped blade.

Spung A purse.

Spur
1. Short supporting timber.
2. Foot device to prick a horse to urge it forward.

Spur Royal Gold coin minted under James I, worth fifteen shillings; a device on one side resembled a *rowel, hence the name.

Spurging Tub Tub for fermenting beer.

Spurling Type of sprat; may also refer to the nets used to catch them.

Spy Glass Early type of telescope.

Squab
1. Originally thick, soft cushions, but later applied to sofas or couches.
2. Club like feet on furniture.

Squirm Yarn was placed on a squirm when it came from being spun; it was wound from the squirm to the warping bar.

Stack
1. Hay, straw, grain in the sheaf, *etc.,* piled into a square or circular stack and thatched to protect it from the weather.
2. A measure of coal and wood.

Stack Garth Rick or stack yard.

Stack Stones *Staddle stones used as the base of a *rick staddle.

Stackwood A load of faggot firewood.

Staddle Raised platform on which ricks were built, to keep the crop off the ground and protect it against rodents.

Staddle Stone Tapered stone pillar with a cap, in the shape of a mushroom; a number were needed to form a *staddle.

Staff Hook Long-handled hook or sickle, used to cut peas and beans, and to trim hedges.

Stag A male animal in its prime, especially an unbroken stallion or a young *ox.

Stained Canvas, Cloth *Painted cloth

Stake
1. Small, moveable anvil.
2. Timber or plank supporting a hay rick.
3. Steel clothing; armour. (Oxf)

Stalder Stool on which casks were placed.

Stale The handle of a broom or other implement.

Stall Hive, or stock of bees for a hive.

Stall Cloth Bench-cloth, especially for a bench in front of a shop on which goods are displayed for sale.

Stamen The warp thread of a textile fabric.

Stamin A coarse worsted fabric.

Stammel A coarse worsted cloth, or *linsey woolsey, usually dyed red; the colour itself.

Stammet Cloth, perhaps fulled, and usually dyed red.

Stamp Instrument for making holes in horse-shoes.

Stamped Paper Paper vellum or parchment on which a duty introduced in 1694 had been levied, and which was stamped accordingly.

Stamper Copper mallet for beating felt placed on a *block into the shape of a hat.

Stand
1. Stall for a horse or ox. (Lin)
2. Wooden vessel to hold *small beer. (Lan)

Stand Cratch, Heck Fodder rack, standing on four posts, for use in the field or yard.

Standard
1. A measuring vessel.
2. A tall candlestick.
3. A stand, on a single pillar, with a branched foot, used as the base for a washing basin, a dressing table, a candlestick, *etc.*
4. Permanent fixtures and fittings to remain in a house, treated as inalienable chattels.
5. A chest used when travelling. (Dby)

Stander, Standert
1. A frame for supporting barrells, pails, kits, *etc.*
2. A barrel set on its end, an open tub.

Standing Fixed.

Standing Bedstead A high bedstead on legs under which a *truckle bed could be rolled; a four-poster with a *tester, curtains, and *valance.

Standing Cupboard A wardrobe that stands on its base.

Standing Desk *Desks with sloping lids and legs.

Standing Press *Standing Cupboard.

Standish A stand or tray for writing materials; an ink-stand.

Stang
1. A wooden beam or bar, which might have various different uses, e.g. the side of a cart, the beam to which the harness is attached, the side piece of a ladder, to hang *flitches on, *etc.*
2. An eel spear.
3. A rood of land. (Lin; Yks)

Staple A thread of wool, especially as regards its length and fineness.

Start A handle. (Lin)

Statute Lace Lace woven according to statute for those forbidden to wear foreign lace.

Stavesacre A plant whose seeds were used as an emetic, or to destroy vermin.

Stays Corsets.

Steane
1. Clay vessel with two handles or ears, used for storing food or liquids.
2. Box carrying stones used to press down on curds in cheese-making; a cheese-press. (Dor)
3. An earthenware drinking vessel.

Steddy *Stithy.

Stee Ladder. (Northern)

Steech Stooks: a dozen or so sheaves stacked in a field. (Dev)

Steed *Bedstead.

Steel
1. A sharp cutting tool or weapon.
2. A bar or rod of steel used for sharpening knives.

Steel Cap Skull cap of steel worn by infantry soldiers.

Steel Glass Glass backed with steel to make a mirror, or perhaps a mirror made of polished steel.

Steel Mill
1. A *malt mill.
2. Device for producing a stream of sparks by rotating a steel disk against a flint.

Steelyard A type of balance, used particularly for weighing meat. The balance had unequal arms; the counterweight was slid along the longer one until equilibrium was reached and the weight of the object measured.

Steep Lead, Steeping Vat Vat for steeping, used in brewing, dyeing, or clothes washing.

Steer Young castrated bull; an ox.

Steg A gander. (Yks)

Stell A stand for barrels; trestles.

Startup Originally a type of boot or shoe worn by rustics that 'started' in the middle of the leg; subsequently, gaiters.

Stew
1. Hatter's drying room.
2. Heated room; room with a fireplace.
3. Cooking vessel or *cauldron.

Steyney Earthenware pan.

Stibium Black antimony, used as a cosmetic for blackening the eyebrows, or as an emetic or poison.

Stechados French lavender, used medicinally.

Stick A measure of the length of a roll of fabric imported from Flanders.

Stiddy *Stithy.

Stile
1. *Still (2).
2. Upright post or bar in *wainscot panelling.

Stile Iron Iron for pressing clothes.

Stiled Dog Iron fire-dog. (Dev)

Stiletto A short dagger, with a thick blade in proportion to its length.

Still, Stilt
1. Stand for a barrell or tub.
2. Apparatus for distilling.
3. *Cooler.

Still House Room or building with a *still (2).

Stillatory *Still (2), or place for distilling.

Stilliard *Steelyard

Stirk Young bullock or heifer, usually one to two years old.

Stitch Sheaves stacked temporarily in the harvest field.

Stithy Blacksmith's anvil.

Stock
1. The block of wood on which a butcher cuts his meat, a fishmonger cuts fish, or on which food is prepared.
2. A stand, frame, or ledge for placing churns, basins, etc.
3. A trough or basin.
4. Collective name for a tradesman's goods, or for a farm's animals.
5. A swarm of bees.
6. The heavy part of a tool, implement or weapon, e.g. the frame of a spinning wheel, the wooden portion of a gun, the handle of a whip.
7. The hub of a wheel.
8. A stiff, close-fitting neckcloth.

Stock Axe Similar to a pick axe, but with the blades flattened for cutting.

Stock Bed *Bed stock

Stock Card Wool *card fastened to a stock(6) or support, thus leaving both hands free to comb.

Stock Fish Fish, especially cod, dried without salting.

Stock Lock Lock for an outer door, fitted in a wooden case.

Stock Stool Stool made from a tree-trunk or large log.

Stocks and Blocks Odds and ends.

Stomacher Ornamental covering for a woman's chest, worn under the lattice of a *bodice; bib of an apron; a type of waistcoat for men.

Stone, Stonige, Stoning, Stony Made of stone; in the South-West, usually moorstone.

Stone Blue Compound of indigo and starch or whiting, used in laundrying.

Stone Bow Cross-bow or catapult that shoots stones, used to kill birds or small animals.

Stone Jug Jug made of stoneware.

Stoned Horse Stallion.

Stool Chair Chair without arms.

Stool Pan Pan for a *close barrel.

Stool Work Tapestry work made on a stool.

Stoop Post or pillar.

Stooper A wedge used to tilt a barrel.

Stop Small well bucket or milk pail.

Stopping Stick Wooden block inserted into a shoe to hold its materials in place whilst the cobbler works on it.

Storax A fragrant gum resin.

Store
1. The stock or tools of a tradesman.
2. Beasts kept for fattening.

Story A painting or sculpture representing a historical subject.

Stot A young ox or heifer. (Northern)

Stouk Basket Basket with a handle.

Stoup
1. Bucket or pail, usually wooden. (Northern)
2. Drinking cup, flagon or tankard; usually deep and narrow.
3. Post; gatepost. (Northern)

Stove Grate or foot-warmer, burning charcoal.

Stover Winter food for cattle.

Stow A heated chamber or room.

Stowell Stool.

Straik A measure of timber.

Strait Cloth of a narrow width, as opposed to *broad cloth.

Strake A section of the metal rim of a cart wheel.

Strakine, Streke Bundle of hemp, flax, *etc.* when dressed

Strang Shaft. (Lan)

Straw Chair Chair made of woven straw.

Straw Chip Basket made of straw. (Dby)

Strawen Made of straw.

Stress Roof timber. (Dur)

Strickle
1. Wooden board covered with sand or emery; used to sharpen knives or sickles.
2. The implement by which a measure of grain was levelled to the rim of the measure; the amount so measured.

Strike
1. A measure of corn, from a half to four bushels, varying by locality; a measuring vessel of this capacity.
2. A bundle of hemp or flax.

String Reins by which the ploughman controlled his oxen, or the rider his horse.

String of Land *Selion: the basic unit of ploughing. (Sfk)

Strip Ornamental attire worn around the neck, chiefly by women.

Stripe Any spoil or waste made on land by a tenant to the detriment of his land, e.g. making land barren by continual ploughing. (Hrt)

Strong Waters Alcoholic spirits such as gin used as a beverage.

Stub A short thick nail, especially an old horse-shoe nail, used for making stub-iron.

Stud
1. Large nail heads or bosses for harness decoration and/or protection.
2. An upright timber between principal posts in a timber-framed wall.

Stuff Worsted cloth without nap or pile; often dyed, patterned or printed; also used for any fabric.

Stump Bedstead *Bedstead without posts and *tester.

Stun(d)
1. Half barrel or tub used in the dairy. (Sal)
2. Earthenware jar. (Sal)

Sture *Steer.

Style Iron Pointed instrument used for marking. (Ham)

Suck The part of the plough which cuts underneath the slice of earth cut by the *culter.

Sucking Pig Piglet: new-born or very young pig.

Succade, Suckett Fruit preserved in sugar, either in syrup or candied.

Suffrage Intercessory prayers; prayers for the soul of the departed.

Sugar Box, Chest Chest or box for storing sugar.

Suit A shroud or coffin.

Sull, Sullow Plough. (South-West)

Sumach A preparation derived from the sumach tree used in tanning and dyeing leather; also used medicinally.

Summer Tree
1. Principal beam of a floor.
2. One of the principal timbers of a wagon's bottom and sides.

Sumpter Cloth Cloth placed under the saddle of a *sumpter horse; frequently ornamented.

Sumpter Horse Horse used for carrying goods on its back: a pack horse.

Surces, Surcingle Girth for a horse: the straps that keep the saddle or pack in its place.

Surety Person offering a guarantee on behalf of someone else.

Surplice
1. A loose white vestment worn by clergy.
2. A labourer's smock frock. (Dor)

Surrogate Clergyman authorised to issue marriage licences on behalf of a bishop.

Surtout Man's great coat or overcoat.

Suter *Shooter.

Swaddle Bands Narrow lengths of cloth wound round a new-born baby.

Swage
1. An ornamental moulding, grooving, mount, or border on a candlestick, basin, *etc.,* hence 'swaged'

2. A blacksmith's tool for bending cold metal to the required shape; metal die or stamp for shaping wrought iron by hammering or pressure.

Swaler Wholesale dealer in corn and provisions. (Lan)

Swarf Iron filings or shavings; waste iron from a blacksmith.

Swath Bands *Swaddle Bands.

Swathe Rake A rake with wooden teeth and a long handle, used in hay-making to form swathes or rows.

Sway, Sway Pole A crane or bar over a fire, from which pots could be hung.

Sweap Pump handle.

Sweat Cloth
1. A cloth for horses.
2. Handkerchief.

Sweet Powder Perfumed powder used as a cosmetic.

Sweet Water A liquid perfume or scent.

Sweatmeat Confectionary, e.g. sugared nuts, fruit flavoured sugary sweets, *etc.*

Sweetwood Timber from various West Indian trees.

Swift Reel on which a skein of yarn is placed to be wound off onto the bobbins of a loom.

Swine Form A rough, wide, heavy, form on which pigs were killed.

Swine Stock Wooden collar for a pig, to prevent it pushing through hedges or straying. (Lin/Yks)

Swing Glass Mirror suspended on pivots.

Swingle, Swingle Hand Implement resembling a sword for beating and scraping flax or hemp to cleanse it of impurities; hence 'swingling'.

Swingle Stock
1. Wooden box or trough into which cloth was placed to be beaten by the *swingle.
2. *Swingletree.

Swingletree On a plough or cart, *etc.,* the cross-bar pivoted in the middle, to which traces are attached, and which swings at the horse's or oxen's heels.

Sylde Bay or compartment.

Sylinge *Sealed.

T

Tabby Silk taffeta, originally striped, but later applied to silks of uniform colour, waved or watered.

Tabernacle Canopied recess or niche in a wall or pillar, perhaps ornate, to house the statue of a saint or other image.

Table
1. Payment for board and lodging.
2. *Table Board.

Table Basket *Voider (1).

Table Board The top or board of a trestle table, but not its *frame.

Table Carpet Table cloth.

Table Chair *Chair Table.

Table Form Trestles.

Tableman One of the pieces used in games played at table.

Tablet
1. A panel or slab, usually of wood, on which there is a picture or inscription.
2. A tile or slab used in roofing or flooring.
3. Loft. (Gls)

Tach, Tach Hook Device for fastening clothes together, e.g. a clasp, buckle, eye and hook, *etc.*

Tack
1. A hanging shelf.
2. Clasp or board for a cheese container.
3. Pasture for cattle or horses hired out.

Tackle Equipment, especially a horse's harness, *etc.*

Taffeta In the seventeenth century, a thin plain woven glossy silk, usually with warp and weft of different colours.

Taffeta Sarcenet Very fine *taffeta, used for linings.

Tag An ornamental pendant; a tassel.

Tag Tail Tagged: having a tail tipped with white or other distinctive colour.

Tagged Out of condition or appearing to be unhealthy.

Tail Male The entailment of an estate to male heirs; each heir held an estate for life only, and therefore could not dispose of their family's long-term interest in it.

Take *Intake.

Tallage A tax or aid imposed by feudal lords upon their tenants; by the 16th century, a municipal levy.

Tallet
1. Hay-loft with an open front, formed by boarding joists over a stable.
2. *Tally.

Tallet Poles Poles supporting a hay-loft.

Tallow Hard animal fat used for making candles, soap, dressing leather, *etc.*

Tallow Cake A large ball of *tallow for use of a *chandler (2).

Tally A rod of wood, notched to indicate the amounts of debts or repayments. They were cleft along the notches, so that both creditor and debtor could retain one half as proof of the amount owed.

Talwood Wood of a specific size cut for fuel.

Tamarine A woollen cloth.

Tambo Frame A drum or frame on which linen was stretched when being embroidered. (Wor)

Tambour Chain stitch embroidery worked with a specially designed needler on a tambour frame.

Tammy A fine worsted cloth of good quality, with a highly glazed finish; originally made in Tamworth, Staffordshire.

Tan Garth Tanning yard.

Tang Large girth used to fasten *panniers or loads on a pack saddle. (Gls)

Tank, Tankard Drinking vessel with a handle and lid, perhaps made of wooden staves and hooped.

Tanner One who tans hides to make leather.

Tap Borer Tool for boring tap or bung-holes.

Tapestry Decorated woven fabric used for wall hangings, curtains, *etc.*

Taper Large wax candle used for ecclesiastical purposes, and often paid for by executors to stand beside a coffin.

Tare The seed of a vetch common in seed corn, and which grows as a weed amongst the corn.

Target A light round shield or buckler.

Tassel Teazle, used to raise the nap on cloth.

Taster Small shallow cup, often silver, for sampling wine.

Tavern Cellar, usually a shop or workshop; cupboard. Not necessarily underground.

Taw A whip or lash.

Tawed Made into white leather by steeping in *alum and salt.

Tawer A *tanner; one who prepares white leather.

Tawny A woollen cloth, light yellowish brown in colour (or the colour itself).

Tea Kettle Lamp A small spirit lamp which could be placed under a tea kettle to keep it warm.

Team
1. Collective noun for a set or group of things.
2. Chains used with harness, by which horses or oxen pull their plough, cart, *etc.*

Tear
1. Fine, or delicate, used especially of flour and hemp.
2. Dressed hempen fibres for making into sheets.

Teasel Plant with a burr-like head, used to raise the nap in finishing woollen cloth.

Teath *Cards.

Ted The action of turning and spreading new mown hay to dry.

Teg Yearling sheep before their first shearing.

Telle *Till.

Temple, Temple Head Device to keep cloth stretched on the loom during weaving.

Temps, Temse A fine sieve, riddle, or *searce (1), used for *bolting flour, and often made of *hair; also used in brewing and the woollen trades.

Tend, Tene Tine: the prong or tooth of a *harrow.

Tenement Land holding, perhaps with a house; a dwelling place.

Tennet Tenon or back saw; saw with a strong metal back.

Tent A low-alcohol red Spanish wine, often used sacramentally.

Tent Bed Small four-poster bed with an arched canopy and covered sides.

Tenter Wooden frame on which cloth was hung to dry after milling; it had to dry evenly and without stretching or shrinking.

Tenter Hook Hook or bent nail on a *tenter for holding the edges of the cloth in place; they are set closely together.

Tester Flat canopy of a four-poster bed, made of wood and/or cloth, often carved, and supported on the bed posts or suspended from the ceiling.

Tew Tool; implement.

Tew Iron
1. *Tuyere.
2. A blacksmith's long pincers, with which he draws iron from the forge.

Tewer *Tuyere.

Tewtaw Implement for breaking hemp or flax; a *hatchell. (West Midlands)

Thames *Hames.

Thatch Rake Implement with curved teeth used to straighten thatch when it is being laid on a roof.

Thatching Comb A narrow strip of wood studded with nails, used to comb out short pieces of straw from the thatch.

Theal A plank or board of wood; *deal.

Theave Young female sheep which has not lambed.

Themell Thimble.

Theorbo A large lute with a double neck and two sets of tuning strings, the lower for the melody, the upper for base.

Thill Wooden shaft of a cart.

Thill Bell The chain between the shaft-horse's collar and the tugs of the cart-shaft.

Thill Gear Shaft harness.

Thill Hames *Hames. (Lan)

Thin Drink Small beer.

Third The third part of a husband's personal and/or real property, given to his widow during her widowhood.

Thirdendeal A third of a tun; the third part of anything.

Thixel An *adze.

Thole A pin used to fasten a shaft to a cart.

Thrall A stand or frame for barrels or pots, on which they may be tilted.

Thrave A measure of unthrashed corn, or of hay, rushes, *etc.,* varying in different localities, but often two stooks of twelve sheaves each. (Northern)

Thread Edging, Thread Lace Edging or lace made of linen or cotton thread, rather than silk.

Threshel Flail for threshing grain.

Thrinter Three years old.

Thripple
1. Chain tug leading from the collar of the horse to the shafts of the cart or *wain (etc.) (Sal).
2. Moveable sides of a cart, which could be extended to allow it to carry a greater load than would otherwise be possible.

Throck The wooden beam on which the blade of a plough is mounted.

Throw A lathe on which wood is turned.

Thrower Knife used for cleaning *laths and hurdles.

Thrown
1. Wood turned on a lathe, rather than 'joined'.
2. Pots shaped on a potter's wheel.
3. Silk twisted into thread.

Thrum(b) The loose ends or fringe of warp-threads left when the web has been cut off; hence cloth or cushions with tassles or fringes is 'thrummed'.

Thwart Saw Saw for cutting across timber; a cross-cut saw.

Tick, Ticking Mattress case made of hard linen, and containing *flock or feathers, *etc.*; the cloth used for making the mattress case.

Tickney, Ticknall Ware Coarse brown or black glazed earthenware, originating from Ticknall, Derbyshire.

Tie Wig Wig with the hair gathered at the back and tied with ribbon.

Tierce A measure of capacity, equal to a third of a pipe, or 42 gallons; a cask holding this amount.

Tiffany Semi-transparent French silk or muslin fabric, used in veils.

Till A small closed compartment in a larger box or *desk, to hold money or valuables.

Tiller Bow In a cross-bow, the grooved wooden beam along which the arrow fits for greater precision of aim.

Tilt
1. A covering, or awning of coarse cloth, for a wide variety of purposes, e.g. a wagon or cart, a tent, a saddle cloth, a boat, *etc.*
2. *Tilter.

Tilter Wedges placed under barrels to keep them tilted, in order to empty them without stirring up the dregs.

Tilth Field A ploughed field, ready for sowing.

Ting The strap or *girse which fastens a *pannier to a saddle. (Dev)

Tinker An itinerant craftsman who mends pots, pans, and other metal household utensils.

Tinker's Hammer A light hammer used by a *tinker.

Tinker's Kettle Pot or *cauldron made by a tinker.

Tinnen Made of tin.

Tinsel Rich and sparkling silk fabric, with gold and silver thread.

Tippet Originally a strip of fur or cloth hanging from the sleeve or elbow; subsequently a short cape or cloak covering the neck and shoulders. A clergyman wore a black tippet over his surplice.

Tippler Tavern keeper.

Tire Iron rim of a cart-wheel.

Tissue Thin rich cloth, often interwoven with gold or silver.

Tithe The tenth part of the produce of agriculture *etc.*, to which parochial incumbents were legally entitled.

To-Fall Lean to outbuilding; a *hovel.

Toasting Iron
1. *Salamander. (Gls)
2. Bread toaster.
3. Roasting iron for small pieces of meat, incorporating a small drip pan.

Tobacco Tongs A light pair of tongs with a spring between its arms, used to pick up embers to light tobacco.

Tod Measure of weight, usually 28 lbs, but varying locally, used in the wool trade.

Toft A homestead or *messuage; land on which a house has formerly stood.

Tog, Toggle The two small handles of a scythe. (Dev)

Tog Withy The *withies or bands which attached the *swingle tree to the head of the plough or cart, *etc.*

Token A coin issued by a tradesman as a substitute for coins of the realm, when the latter were scarce.

Tone *Tend.

Tongue Tree The pole of a wagon or ox-cart. (Dev)

Top Bundle of combed wool ready for spinning; slivers of wool fibre produced by the comb in manufacturing woollen cloth.

Torch In a church, a processional candle; often used for funerals.

Tortery, Tortree Part of a horse's harness. (Sal)

Tottle Vessell for boiling. (War)

Touch Box A box for gunpowder; part of a musketeer's equipment. It might also be similar to a tinder-box, but using touch-wood, which is a soft white highly inflammable substance.

Tow
1. Either uncleaned wool, or the shorter, coarser fibres of hemp or flax, which have been separated by heckling from the longer threads, and are ready for spinning. Hence towen, made of tow.
2. *Traces, chains or plough-lines.

Tow Comb Comb for separating fibres of hemp or flax.

Towed Yarn Flaxen or hempen yarn from which the *tow has been removed.

Towel
1. Table napkin.
2. *Tuyere.

Towel Stick A cudgel.

Town A settlement; often means the parish, although a single farmstead or a hamlet might also be meant.

Traces Ropes, chains or leather straps by which a horse or oxen's collar is linked to the *swingletree.

Trag *Drag (4). (Sts)

Trail Rake Horse-drawn rake. (Ntt)

Trail Steed Type of *sled cart. (Northern)

Train Rope for dragging a plough or harrow. (Nfk)

Train Oil Oil from whale blubber, similar to *tallow, used by clothiers and soap makers.

Trained Band Local militia force.

Trea A sieve. (Sal)

Train Gown Gown with a train at the rear, worn by the upper classes on formal occasions; the train was sometimes carried by a page or train-bearer.

Tram
1. The shafts of a cart wagon or wheel-barrow.
2. A wooden framework or stand on which barrels and tubs could be stood.

Trammell
1. A long narrow fishing net with floats and sinkers, consisting of two 'walls' of wide-mesh netting, between which is a net of fine mesh.
2. A fowler's net.
3. A hobble for a horse, to prevent it kicking or straying.
4. An instrument for drawing ellipses.
5. Rings, links, hooks or bar over a fire-place, from which pots could be hung at various heights.

Tran *Trine

Trandle *Dough kever.

Tranklement *Hustlements. (Dby)

Transom
1. Mattress or bolster.
2. Cross-beam of stone or wood across the top of a door or window.

Trap Reel Used in conjunction with a spinning wheel to measure yarn into hanks or skeins. (Ess)

Trash Household oddments not worth valuing.

Tray
1. A wooden hurdle, often used for folding sheep. (Lin; Yks)
2. Screen for sifting malt from a kiln. (Sal)

Treadle Wheel Spinning wheel, which was operated from a sitting position by means of a treadle.

Tree A stave or piece of wood, especially one that has been made into something, e.g. an *axletree, a *swingletree, a roof-tree, *etc.*

Tree Chain Chain attached to a *tree, i.e. the wooden part of a plough.

Treen Ware Wooden table ware such as bowls or *platters, usually *thrown rather than sawn, made out of single pieces of wood.

Tregar Linen fabric from Treguier, Brittany.

Trencher A thin, flat, wooden or pewter *platter from which food was eaten. It might be hollowed on both sides, so that meat could be eaten from one side, and a second course from the other. It often had a hole in the rim for salt, and might be square or round. Often made of sycamore. The name derives from the earliest form of plate, which was a thick slice of bread, in French 'tranche'.

Trencher Salt Large salt cellar.

Trendle
1. A large, oval, tub or trough, used for brewing or in the dairy.
2. A lump of wax. (Bdf)
3. A small wheeled truck or cart; see also *trundle. (Dev)

Trenket
1. Iron heel put on a shoe.
2. A shoe-makers knife.

Trental A set of thirty successive masses for the soul of the departed, perhaps all said on the same day.

Trepan Surgical crown-saw, for cutting small pieces of bone from the skull.

Tress The rope or chain *etc.,* by which the *swingletree was connected to the collar of a draught animal.

Trestle
1. The detachable legs (always in pairs) which support a table board.
2. A long bench or form. (Dor)

Trimmer A canopy.

Trindleware *Treen.

Trine Thirteen *felloes, or twenty-five spokes: the wheelwright's stock in trade.

Trippet, Trivet Three-footed metal tripod for standing a pot over a fire; subsequently a metal bracket to hook on the bars of a grate.

Trochisk Pastille or lozenge; a medical tablet.

Trolly A kind of lace. (Dev)

Trose Bill Hedger's hatchet. (Wor)

Trough A narrow, open, v-shaped tank or vessel, made of wood, stone, metal or earthenware, often a fixture used for washing, kneading, brewing, *etc.,* in the household.

Trouse Close-fitting breeches or drawers, covering the buttocks and thighs, worn by men; knee breeches.

Trow *Trough.

Trowel A culinary ladle or slice.

Troy Weight The standard unit of measurement for weighing precious metals.

Truckle Castor wheel.

Truckle Bed Low bedstead on castors or slides, without a head-board, which could be rolled or pushed under a *standing bedstead during the day time. Usually used by servants and children.

Trumpery Items of little value, rubbish.

Trundle, Trunnill Bed *Truckle Bed.

Truss
1. *Trouse.
2. A bundle of hay or straw.

Truss Bed Portable bed which could be taken apart and trussed up for travelling, or perhaps a framed bed, using 'truss' in its architectural sense.

Trussing Silk Silk made into laces for lacing *doublet and *hose.

Try Sieve or screen for sifting.

Tub A wooden container, usually hooped and staved, capable of holding about half a barrel of water; if more it is a *vat; if less a *turnel.

Tuck A slender pointed sword: a rapier.

Tucker Person engaged in the fulling and dressing of cloth: a fuller or cloth-finisher.

Tucker's Shears Shears used in cloth finishing.

Tuft Mockado *Mockado decorated with small tufts of wool.

Tug, Tugwithy The *traces connecting the horse's collar to the *swingletree, or the rope or chain connecting the *swingletree to the head of the plough.

Tuition Guardianship or upbringing.

Tuke
1. Canvas, or a finer fabric used to line garments.
2. *Tick. (Gls)

Tumbler Drinking cup with a rounded bottom, so that it could not be put down until its contents had been drunk; often of silver or gold.

Tumbling Churn Revolving barrel containing emery, in which castings were cleaned by friction. (Sfk)

Tumbrel
1. High-sided tipping cart on two wheels, often used to cart manure.
2. Frame for holding fodder in fold yards or the open field.
3. Counterpoise for raising a well bucket. (Lin)

Tun
1. A large cask for ale, beer, wine, *etc.,* holding 252 gallons, 2 *pipes, or 4 *hogsheads; the largest barrel in common use.
2. A *mashing fat or *gyle tun.
3. A cup or small drinking vessel.
4. *Tundish.

Tunbridge Ware Small wooden objects lavishly decorated with parquetry patterns, made at Tunbridge Wells in the late 17th century.

Tundish Wooden vessel with a tube at the base which fitted into the bung-hole of a cask or barrel, and thus formed a funnel.

Tunicle Ecclesiastical vestment, worn by sub-deacons over the alb at celebrations of the eucharist.

Tunnel
1. A funnel.
2. A *turnel.

Tup
1. A ram. (Lan)
2. The head of a hammer. (Sal)

Tupping Hurdle Hurdle to confine a ram. (i.e. a *tup)

Turf Peat or cut turf used for fuel.

Turkes Precious stone from Persia of sky blue or light green colour, and almost opaque or translucent.

Turkey, Turkey Work Cross-stitched woollen *carpet on a canvas backing, with a deep pile, woven from richly coloured yarn in the Turkish fashion, used as a covering for chairs, cushions, *etc.*

Turkey Colour Azure.

Turkey Leather Leather tawed with oil.

Turling Bed *Truckle Bed

Turmeric Powder made from the aromatic root of an East Indian plant of the ginger family, used as a dye, a spice and medicinally.

Turn
1. Spinning wheel, spindle.
2. Churn. (Gls)
3. Winding gear for a well or grindstone. (Dby)

Turn Barrel Winding apparatus at a mine.

Turn Up Bed Bed that can be folded up when not in use.

Turncoat
1. A reversible coat.
2. Anything that changes its appearance or colour.

Turned Furniture, especially chairs and tables, which has been turned on a lathe.

Turnel
1. A shallow oval tub or half-barrel, used for salting meat, kneading bread, making cheese, *etc.*
2. The windlass over a well.
3. A ring turning on a swivel, a terret, used on horse harness.

Turners Work Furniture, *etc.,* turned on a lathe.

Turnsole Violet-blue or purple colouring matter, used in food and wine, and later as a pigment.

Turves Turf or peat used as fuel.

Tutaw *Tewtaw.

Tutor Guardian.

Tuyere The nozzle of a blacksmith's bellows, through which air is blasted to the base of his furnace or forge.

Twibill Axe or mattock with two cutting edges.

Twiggen, Twigger Basket work; made of twigs, wicker, rush, *etc.*

Twilight
1. Box containing toiletries. (Wor)
2. Rich covering for a dressing table. (Wor)

Twill, Twilly A coarse linen fabric, in which the weft passes alternately over one warp thread and then under two or more threads, producing a lined effect; often used for bed coverings.

Twill Wheel *Quill Torn.

Twilt *Quilt.

Twin Doors The entry doors of a house, at opposite ends of the cross passage.

Twinter Cattle, sheep or colts of two years old.

Twist Lace *Bobbin lace.

Tye *Bed tick.

U

Ullage The amount of wine or liquor by which a cask or bottle falls short of being full.

Umber A brown earth used as a pigment; its colour.

Unbraked Used of hemp: uncombed.

Underback Vessel placed beneath a *mashing fat to collect the raw *wort.

Unguent Ointment or salve.

Untall Thread *Outnal

Unwatered Camlet Plain *camlet, i.e. 'unwatered'.

Up Muck Dung piled in heaps in the field ready for spreading. (Sts)

Upper Stock The upper and wider part of the *hose.

Ure
1. Lead ore.
2. Ewer.

Use Money 'put to use' is earning interest.

Uster *Worsted. (Dev)

Usclement *Husslement.

Uting Vat Vat for soaking or 'uting' barley before making malt.

Utter To offer goods for sale.

Uxor Wife (Latin).

V

Valance Short curtain or border around the canopy or frame of a bedstead, or above a window; subsequently used to describe the border of any drapery.

Valencia A mixed fabric with a woollen weft and silk or linen weft.

Valley *Felloe.

Vamp That part of the *hose which covers the foot; stocking or sock.

Vance Roof Garret, attic, loft. (Nfk; Sfk)

Vandelas, Vandloes A strong coarse canvas used for sails, made in Le Vendelais, Brittany.

Vantage Profit, gain, advantage.

Vapour Bath Form of Turkish bath used in the 18th c.

Vara A Spanish linear measure, i.e. 33 inches.

Vat A cask or tun, capable of holding more than half a barrel of liquid, used in brewing and cheese-making, *etc.*

Vellies *Felloe.

Velour *Velvet, or imitation velvet.

Velvet A silk fabric with a short, dense smooth pile.

Ven Rake Musk rake. (Dev)

Venice Glass Fine drinking glass or looking glass from Merano, close to Venice.

Venice Turpentine Turpentine exuded from the bark of the white larch.

Verdigris Copper salt used as a green pigment in dyeing, formed by the action of caustic acid on copper; also used medicinally.

Verdingal *Farthingale.

Verdure Rich tapestry decorated with representations of trees and shrubs; vivid green colour.

Verinas Superior rolled tobacco, originally produced in Varinas, Venezuela.

Verjuice The acid juice of crab apples (i.e. crab apple vinegar), or other sour fruit such as green walnuts and unripe grapes; kept in hogsheads, and much used in cooking and for dosing animals.

Vermilion Red crystalline mercuric sulphide, used as a brilliant scarlet pigment, and in the manufacture of sealing wax.

Vessell Staves The pieces of wood forming the sides of a barrel or vat.

Vestment A garment worn by a priest during services and ceremonies.

Vetch Leguminous plants such as clover and lucerne, used as cattle fodder; also used for bedding.

Vice
1. Screw stopper; the tap of a vessel.
2. Device or mechanical contrivance by which something is worked.

Victualler One who sells food and drink; an innkeeper.

Victuals at the Roof Meat and other foodstuff hung from the roof or ceiling, inaccessible to rodents.

Vintner A wine merchant.

Viol A stringed musical instrument played with a bow; it had between five and seven strings.

Virgate An English land measure, varying in size in different localities, but often thirty acres.

Virginal A keyed musical instrument, set in a box or case without legs; similar to a *spinet.

Visor That part of a helmet protecting the face, capable of being raised and lowered.

Vitry Canvas cloth originally made in Vitré, Brittany.

Vizard Mask with holes for eyes, nose and mouth, worn to conceal identity, to protect the skin from sun-light, and by ladies at the theatre.

Voider, Voiding Basket
1. A metal tray, basket or pail used for disposing of the scraps at meals, or for removing dirty plates *etc.,* from the table.
2. A large wicker basket, usually used for dirty clothes.

Voiding Knife A wooden utensil like a knife, for cleaning the remnants of food from a table.

Volmonger Fellmonger: a dealer in hides, especially sheep-skins. (Con)

Vowess A widow vowed to chastity for the rest of her life.

W

Wad Woad: a blue dye-stuff.

Wadfat Woad vat.

Wadmal A coarse thick woollen material, used to line horse collars and for rough types of clothing.

Wafering Iron
1. Used for making crisp cakes and wafers, it consisted of two iron plates between which the paste was laid.
2. Rope or tie for securing a load on a cart.

Wagon A strong, open, four-wheeled vehicle for carting hay, corn, *etc.,* and furnished with *raves.

Wain A *wagon used for agricultural purposes; most had four wheels, but the two wheeled variety was common in some areas, e.g. Cornwall, Lancashire, Yorkshire.

Wain Blade Shaft of the *wain.

Wain Clout *Clout (1).

Wainscot Wooden panelling lining walls, usually of oak; also applied to panelling on furniture.

Waistcoat A short garment worn on the upper part of the body, usually beneath a *gown, but so as to be seen; the earliest waistcoats were often elaborate and costly, and not necessarily without sleeves.

Waiter A salver or small tray; a dumb waiter.

Walker Fuller; one who fulls cloth.

Walkers Earth Fuller's earth, used to clean cloth.

Wall Bed Bed fixed to a wall, sometimes with doors; it could be folded up when not in use.

Wallet Bag for holding provisions or clothes on a journey; a pedlar's pack.

Wampty *Surces, surcingle.

Wanded Wickerwork was made from wands, i.e. young shoots of willow. Hence 'wanded'.

Want Staff Moling spear, to catch moles.

Wantow, Wanty Rope or *surces used to secure a pack on a pack saddle, or a load on the back of a horse.

War Saddle Saddle for a cavalryman.

Warden Tree A variety of pear.

Ware
1. Spring; hence 'ware-corn', i.e. spring corn. (Dur; Yks)
2. A collective term for the trade goods of a merchant, pedlar, tradesmen, *etc.;* merchandise.

Warming Pan Shallow container of brass or copper, with a long handle, filled with hot embers, used to 'iron' beds, and thus warm them.

Warp The threads that run lengthwise in the loom, at right angles to the weft, through which the latter must pass in the process of weaving.

Warp Fat, Warping Vat Vat or trough in which the weaver places balls of yarn when running them off for warping.

Warping Bar, Frame, Stock, Wough The frame or bar on which the yarn was wound to form a *warp before transfer to the loom.

Warping Tree Frame used in cloth-making.

Wash Brewery waste used as food for swine.

Washing Ball A ball of soap.

Washing Maid Wooden staff for pounding clothes when washing them in a tub.

Washing Stock Bench on which clothes were laid and beaten with a bat; stand for a wash tub.

Washing Stone, Vat Tub or stone trough for washing clothes.

Wassail Board A large board for mixing and storing liquor, into which cups could be dipped for drinking healths.

Watch and Ward The duties of a night watchman.

Watch Bill *Bill (1) used by watchman, sometimes of a military type; a *halberd.

Watchet Pale blue cloth; the colour.

Water Bushel Measure for goods such as coal, salt, fruit, *etc.,* sold on board ship. (Ham)

Water Candlestick Vertical tub filled with water, holding a floating candlestick.

Water Chaffer A *chaffer on which water could be heated.

Water Glover, Wet Glover Maker of leather gloves.

Water Plate Plate with a hollow bottom which can be filled with hot water to keep it warm, or perhaps a separate receptacle for hot water placed under a plate for the same purpose.

Watered Silk or other textiles with a wavy lustrous finish.

Watering Stone Drinking trough for animals.

Way Tree *Whipple Tree.

Weanling An animal, usually a calf, being weaned, or just weaned.

Wearing Apparell, Clothes Clothes, *apparell.

Wearing Band Loose turn-over collar for the neck, which succeeded the ruff.

Weather Glass Barometer or temperature gauge.

Weaving Making textile fabric by crossing the *warp and the *weft.

Web
1. Piece of cloth in the process of weaving, or when it has just come off the loom.
2. Large piece of cloth, leather, metal, *etc.*

Webster A weaver.

Wedset A mortgage of land, or its conveyance in satisfaction of a debt, with provision for the debtor to recover it on payment of the debt or performance of some obligation.

Weeting Vat *Uting Vat.

Weft The thread that runs from side to side of the loom, at right angles to the *warp.

Weigh(ing) Back, Baulk, Beam Transverse bar of a balance or set of scales, or perhaps the scales themselves.

Well Drag Three-pronged drag for retrieving the bucket or things dropped in a well. (Dby; Ntt)

Welsh Hook Bill-hook.

Welt A narrow strip of material used to edge or border a garment, perhaps ornamentally.

Wemb(ing) Sheet *Winnowing Cloth

Wen *Wain.

Went A furlong of land; a portion of an open field separated from the rest of the field by some barrier, e.g. a road.

Wet Fish Fresh fish, not dried.

Wet Larder Larder for storing moist or liquid provisions.

Wether A male sheep, especially a castrated ram.

Wether Hog Male sheep before its first shearing.

Wey Standard of dry goods weight; varying in amount according to the commodity being weighed.

Wharl *Quarrel (1).

Whearne *Quern.

Wheat Manchet Loaf or roll of white bread; muffin; hot cake, *etc.*

Wheel Usually a spinning wheel or *turn.

Whelff *Felloe. (Lin; Yks)

Whepe A pruning knife. (War)

Wherry A large four wheeled cart without sides.

Which, Whitch
1. A bin or tub made of split planks of oak wedged and pegged together; a chest, coffer or hutch. Used for storing meal, flour, *etc.*
2. A sieve or wicker strainer. (Wor)

Whiff *Coif (Dev).

Whin Gorse or furze.

Whip Saw
1. Frame saw with a narrow blade for curved work.
2. A long, narrow, two-man saw.

Whipcord Thin, but tough, hempen cord, used for making whips.

Whip Whang A long thin strip of leather used for the lash of a whip. (Lin; Yks)

Whipple Tree, Whipping Tree A free-swinging piece of wood to which the *traces of a plough, harrow, *etc.* were attached; a *swingletree.

Whisk
1. A brush made from leather, twigs, hair, *etc.,* bound together on a stick.
2. A cape or short cloak. (War)

White Candlestick Made of silver.

White Cloth Undyed cloth.

White Coal Wood slit into small pieces dried in a kiln, and turned into charcoal for smelting.

White Grain Wheat, barley, and oats, rather than peas and beans.

White House Dairy.

White Lead Compound of lead carbonate and hydrated oxide of lead, used as a white pigment.

White Leather Horse skin cured with lime; used for parchment and for strong laces, being hard and tough.

White Meat Dairy produce.

White Metal Various alloys coloured light grey.

White Money Silver coin.

White Plate Enamelled tin-plate.

White Salt Salt for household use.

White Silver Silver ware chased or roughened, as opposed to burnished.

White Smith Smith who finished off goods begun by other smiths, e.g. attaching the haft to an axe head, fitting the pieces of a gun together, *etc.*

White Ware White earthenware of good quality.

White Work Cut and slashed lace.

Whitsull *Whitemeat. (Dev)

Whittawer A saddler or glover: one who worked in white leather.

Whiting Bleaching.

Whittle
1. A baby's flannel petticoat; a shawl for women, especially nursing mothers. (South West)
2. A cloak.
3. A large knife; a carving knife or butchers knife. (Northern)

Whye *Quy. (Yks)

Wick An enclosed piece of land, a close, a dwelling place, hamlet, village or dairy farm.

Wick Yarn Yarn used as a wick in candles, lamps, or tapers.

Wicker Pliable twigs, usually willow, used for basket-making.

Wicket A small door or gate beside a larger one, for use when the latter is closed; also any small gate for pedestrians.

Widge Beast A horse. (Dev)

Wig Block Rounded block on which a wig was stored when not in use.

Wimble
1. A gimlet, *auger, or brace, for boring holes.
2. A hay trusser's tool for twisting and plaiting ropes of straw or hay.

Winding Rod or withy for making and repairing a wall or other building work. (Sts)

Winding Blade Spindle for winding thread or yarn.

Wind(ing) Cloth, Sheet
1. *Winnowing Cloth.
2. Shroud in which a body is wrapped for burial.

Windlass Hand operated winding drum, for raising and lowering masts, raising minerals from a pit, raising buckets from a well, *etc.*

Windle
1. A winnowing basket.
2. *Windle Blade.
3. *Windlass.

Windle Blade Spindle for winding a skein of yarn into a ball.

Window Board A shutter.

Window Cloth Cloth used in place of glass for a window.

Window Grate Framework or bar preventing entry through the window.

Window Leaf, Leam Removeable window, including both glass and frame.

Window Lid *Lid.

Window Sheet
1. *Window Cloth.
2. *Winnowing Cloth.

Windsor Chair Chair with a solid seat, the back and legs being spindles, and sometimes with arms.

Wing Iron side piece of a grate.

Wingle *Windle Blade.

Winnowing Cloth, Sheet Winnowing was the process of separating the grain from the chaff after threshing. The grain was sieved or screened in the wind (either natural or created by a winnowing fan). The chaff blew away, but the grain fell on the winnowing sheet.

Winter Corn Wheat or rye, sown in the autumn.

Wiper Handkerchief.

Wisket A strong osier bucket, used in the garden, for animal fodder, and for various other purposes. It had a hole at each end for carrying, rather than a handle.

Withy Willow tree; also applied to its branches, which are very flexible, and were used extensively in basket making, the seats of chairs, for tying or binding, *etc.*

Witney A heavy woollen cloth with a nap, made in Witney, and used for blankets.

Womb The belly piece of a hide used in shoe-making.

Wombing Sheet *Winnowing Cloth.

Womble *Wimble (1).

Wong Unenclosed land in the open field: a group of *selions or strips. (Lin)

Wood Coal Charcoal obtained from wood.

Wood Knife Huntsman's dagger, for cutting up game or as a weapon.

Wool Card *Card.

Wool Comb *Comb (1).

Wool Driver One who buys wool from the producer to sell to the clothmaker.

Wool Wheel Large spinning wheel.

Woolsey Woolly, woollen.

Workhouse Workshop where a trade or craft was carried on; not usually a 'workhouse' in the poor law sense - they mostly came later.

Worm Screw of a screw press.

Worm Seed Seed of a Levantine plant used medicinally to kill intestinal worms.

Worm Tub Tub used in distilling.

Worsted A closely twisted yarn of long staple wool, which has been combed rather than carded to make the fibres lie parallel to each other; the fabric made from this yarn. Originally made in Worstead, Norfolk.

Wort The infusion of malt which becomes beer after fermentation; unfermented beer.

Wort Fat, Store, Trough, Tub Vat *etc.,* in which malt is fermented in beer-making.

Wort Pan Pan used for drawing off the *wort from the *mashing fat in the brewing process.

Worthing Manure; dung. (Lan)

Wrathe *Rave (Yks).

Wring A press, e.g. a *cheese press, *cider press.

Writing A legal document, e.g. a *bill, *obligation, deed, *etc.*

Writing Obligatorie *Obligation.

Wrought Worked, woven, knitted, embroidered, decorated, ornamented, hand-carved, shaped, fashioned, *etc.*

Wynding Sheet, Wynnying Sheett, Wynow Cloth, Wynsheate *Winnowing Cloth.

Wyrgen A very coarse canvas used for baskets. (Oxf)

Y

Yard Arm A spar on a ships mast.

Yard Wand Measuring rod, three feet long.

Yardland The size of a holding in the open fields which might be made up of several strips in various different places; generally 30 acres, but varying by locality. (Midlands)

Yarn Spun fibre of wool, flax, silk, *etc.,* used for weaving or knitting.

Yarn Blade *Windle Blade.

Yate, Yeate Gate.

Year Tub Tub with 'ears' i.e. handles. (Dev)

Yearn Ware Earthenware.

Yeeling, Yelding, Yeln Brewing; variant of *gyle.

Yeld Animals that are barren.

Yellow Griete A type of earthenware pottery. (Chs)

Yeo Ewe.

Yeoman Substantial tenant farmer or freeholder.

Yetling A small iron pot with three feet and a bow handle. (Lin; Yks)

Yewing Suckling. (Yks)

Yoke
1. A curved wooden bar placed over the shoulders of two horses or oxen, to harness them together; they are usually fitted with *ox bows, and there is a central ring or hook for attachment of the *chain or *trace by which their load is drawn.
2. A wooden bar, shaped for the shoulders, from each end of which a bucket is hung, used for ease of carrying.

Yorkshire Thick, coarse cloth made in Yorkshire.

Yrne Iron.